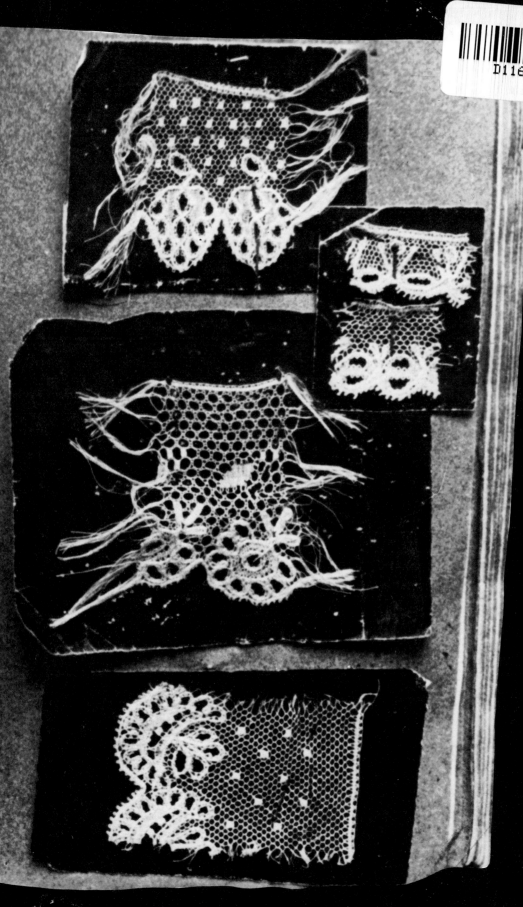

LACE
AND LACE MAKING

Alice-May Bullock

Larousse & Co. Inc., New York, N.Y.

This book is dedicated to my mother and Mo

© Alice-May Bullock 1981
First published 1981

in the United States by
Larousse & Co. Inc.
572 5th Avenue, New York, N.Y. 10036

ISBN 0-88332-261-7
LCCN 81-81037

Printed in Great Britain

Contents

Acknowledgements

My grateful thanks are extended to the following people, without whose help this book would not have been possible.

The librarians of Newmarket Library for their help in obtaining books and preparing library lists.

The students of Norwich Lace School and May Seymour for the loan of their lace work; Patricia Payne for access to her large collection of bobbins and lace; my mother, Evelyn Wood and Violet Spong for the loan of work.

Sean Walsh of the *Bedfordshire Times* for help in my search for lace tells; Bedford Library for access to old Bedfordshire song sheets and lace tells.

Bedford County Record Office for supplying a photograph of the workhouse document in their archives.

Colin Payne, Rod Shaw and Maurice R. Lockey for photographs.

Madge Milton of the Australian Lace Guild, Inez Rodefer of the USA International Old Lacers, Jean Astbury of the Vancouver Lace Club, and the Secretary of the British Lace Guild, all of whom answered my queries promptly and helpfully.

The following museums and collections: Wallace Collection, London (special thanks to Dennis Dolby); British Museum, London; National Portrait Gallery, London; The Museum of London; Tate Gallery, London; Castle Museum, York; Castle Museum, Norwich; Strangers Hall, Norwich; Luton Museum and Art Gallery, Luton (special thanks to Doreen Fudge); National Museum of Ireland, Dublin; BBC Hulton Picture Library, London.

My husband, who patiently read scripts.

1 Lace: What is it?

Dr Johnson described lace or network as 'anything reticulated or decussated at equal distance with interstices between the intersections'. The modern definition of lace is: 'a fine openwork plain or decorated fabric'. However, until the mid-seventeenth century, lace had a quite different meaning. It meant a narrow braid worked on a loom, or a silk or thread cord for drawing two edges together, such as a shoe lace or a stay lace. Before the invention of buttons and other fastenings, garments were held together with laces.

Early lace, of the kind we know today, was classed with gimps, braids and other trimmings as 'passament' or the French *passement*. The French word for lace, *dentelle*, was not used until lace was made with a saw-toothed edge.

Lace can be divided into four main classes: needlepoint, bobbin, other hand-made laces, and machine-made lace.

Purists insist that there are only two genuine laces, needlepoint and bobbin, and that all other laces are merely copies of these. Most people are not concerned with these fine distinctions and accept that laces, whether tatted, knitted, crocheted, netted, knotted, or made by other means, are laces in their own right. Possibly the only exceptions are the darned and tamboured laces such as Limerick, which are, technically, embroidered nets.

Needlepoint, as the name implies, is made with an ordinary sewing needle and single thread. The principal stitch used is buttonhole. Until the sixteenth century, needlepoint lace was called **needlework** lace. Often needlepoint lace is referred to simply as **point**. Point can also mean a bobbin lace stitch such as *point d'esprit* or, again, it can be used to describe a type of bobbin lace such as *Point de Malines* or *Point de Lille*, so it is always wise to check the context in which it is used.

Bobbin Lace, also called **pillow lace**, **bone lace** or **bonework**, is made by twisting and plaiting large numbers of threads together. The threads are wound separately onto individual bobbins and the lace is worked over a parchment pattern on a hard pillow, the threads being held in place by pins. The early bobbins were made of bone, hence the names bone lace or bonework. Use of the pillow gave rise to the name of pillow lace. Since a cushion was often used in the making of needlepoint lace as well, the term bobbin lace is really the best and most accurate.

Mixed lace is a combination of needlepoint and bobbin lace.

Lace makers frequently use French terms in preference to English when referring to the various parts of lace, so French terms as well as English are given here when appropriate.

Lace is made up of two main parts, the solid **pattern**, **mat** or **clothwork** (*toilé*), and the **ground** (*fond*), which is the part that joins the pattern together. The ground can be either regular **network** (*réseau*) or **bride ground**. The former surrounds the pattern and may be a plain or fancy net. Fancy nets are usually characteristic of certain types of lace, such as Lille net, Brussels net, Valenciennes net and Mechlin net. The second, bride ground, is so called because the pattern parts are joined together by little irregular bars (*brides*). Guipure lace is made this way.

Small loops which decorate the edge of lace or the little bars are called **pearls** or **purls** (*picot*). The term **picot** is usually used, pearl being a word more common in the English Midland counties.

Enclosed fancy stitches in the centre of

pattern work are called **fillings** (*jours* or *modes*), and the thick thread used to outline patterns in some laces is called **gimp** (*cordonnet*).

A piece of lace usually has two edges. The one which is sewn on to other material is called the **footing** or the **footside** (*engrêlure*), and the fancy edge is called the **heading** or **headside**.

There are two ways of making bobbin lace. It can be made in one piece, with the ground and the pattern worked together or, as with Honiton and Brussels lace, the motifs can be made separately and the ground worked round them afterwards. Needlepoint lace is nearly always made in the second way, the exception being Hollie point, which is worked in a strip.

Large pieces of lace, whether needlepoint or bobbin, are often made in small sections and sewn together with an invisible **fine joining** stitch (*point de raccroc*). This is used to join the special **droschel** ground in Brussels lace.

Tape laces are made with narrow tape or braid (hand or machine-made) and joined together with bars.

Another way of making lace is by appliqué: hand-made motifs are first made by bobbin or needlepoint, and then appliquéed to machine-made net. The modern Honiton and Brussels laces are made in this way. **Carrickmacross** is also an appliqué lace. Fine muslin instead of hand-made motifs is sewn on to machine-made net.

The very old **lacis** or **filet** lace is darned netting. The net used has a square mesh and the patterns are therefore geometrical. Occasionally linen was also appliquéed onto the net.

This is a brief introduction to the less familiar laces. The more familiar ones such as crochet, tatting and knitting are discussed later in the book.

2 Early Beginnings to the Nineteenth Century

The origins of lace are obscure, and because it is such a fragile fabric many early examples have disintegrated with age. Like many other handicrafts, lace making seems to have begun simply, and gradually to have evolved over the years into its present highly complicated and decorative forms. Needlepoint lace is, almost certainly, a natural development of drawn threadwork and cutwork, while bobbin lace seems to have evolved from the ancient craft of netting, known to man for many thousands of years. No doubt the first primitive nets were used for catching fish and trapping animals for food. As civilization progressed new threads were discovered, and it became possible to make fine, attractive nets suitable for decorating clothing and furnishings.

Network existed in biblical times, and elaborate forms of it, dating back to 1000BC, have been found in the ancient tombs of Egypt. This network was made either of fine linen darned with gold thread, or solely of gold thread. Gold lace was also made in early times by twisting and plaiting gold thread. The oldest pattern that can be traced is a lozenge design. This design was found on fragments of gold lace discovered in a Scandinavian burial ground at Wareham in Dorset. Another good example of antique gold lace was found in the grave of St Cuthbert in Durham Cathedral. Lace as we now know it did not, however, appear until the fifteenth century.

Both Italy and Flanders claim to have invented lace. The Italians maintain that they developed both needlepoint and bobbin lace, but the Flemish also claim that they invented bobbin lace. Both countries can produce some evidence dating from the fifteenth century to support their claims but, unfortunately, it is not until the sixteenth century that we can piece together the history of lace with any degree of accuracy.

From this period not only is there a great deal more documentary evidence available, but European portrait painters of the sixteenth and seventeenth centuries left outstandingly accurate pictorial records of the wealthy wearing their finest and most cherished lace. Sometimes the painter would employ a fellow artist who had a better knowledge of the actual construction of the lace to paint in the more delicate details for him. These beautiful portraits show how lace ornamented contemporary fashions. There are also a number of fascinating documents from this period, such as wardrobe and household accounts and even laundry bills, which indicate how lace was used.

Most of the early lace, before it came into general use, was made by nuns in the convents for church vestments and altar cloths. Because of this, lace making was often called 'nun's work' and the flax thread, 'nun's thread', or 'sister's thread'. Quite a lot of the really old lace which exists today in museums or private collections was found preserved in churches and convents.

Laymen paid vast sums for their lace and they made sure that they had their money's worth by wearing it until it was quite threadbare, leaving little for posterity to inherit and admire. If by chance the lace did outlast its owner it was usually bequeathed to a relative or friend, who wore it into tatters. Quite often the owner was buried in his best lace. As a result, much of the world's most exquisite lace mouldered away in churchyards.

From the pictorial and documentary evidence offered by both Italy and Flanders in advancing their rival claims to have invented lace, it is obvious that the lace depicted or described had been in existence for some time, although no one knows for how long.

The Italians have one very interesting early document which comes from Milan and is dated 1493. It is an inventory of the property of two sisters, Ippolita and Angela Sforza. (The Sforzas were a great ducal family of the fifteenth century.) The inventory lists many items of bed linen and clothing, all trimmed with point and bone lace, as well as network veils and 'half a bundle containing patterns for ladies' work'. It also mentions 'spindle', which is an old name for bobbin (and a name that is used in Belgium today). Another document from Italy, from Ferrara Cathedral and dated 1500, gives details of the price paid for mending and ironing the lace on the priests' vestments. It is obvious from both documents that lace must have been in use for some time.

The Flemish, in their turn, offer a set of wood-cuts dated 1580, illustrating various contemporary occupations. One shows a young girl working on a lace pillow with bobbins, while an older girl works on a vertical frame by her side. We can assume that lace making must have been a common occupation at that date otherwise the artist would not have selected it to represent everyday life.

Today it is generally accepted that Italy developed needlepoint lace, while Flanders perfected bobbin lace. The earliest form of needlepoint lace, known as *Reticella* (or Greek lace) probably originated in Egyptian drawn linen work, and evolved over the centuries into this form of Italian cutwork which was made by completely cutting away the fabric and filling the spaces with patterns made by needle and thread, the early patterns being very geometric. *Reticella* first appeared in Venice, Milan and the Greek Ionian islands in the fifteenth century. The earliest bobbin lace was tape lace. It was supposedly made in Flanders, but the introduction of tape lace has also been attributed to Italy and France.

Lace making spread from Italy and Flanders throughout western Europe and even to America. It spread through merchants and traders, through refugees who fled their homelands as a result of war, persecution or annexation, and through other emigrants who were encouraged to take their skills to neighbouring countries. As a result Europe became a great lace-making centre, each of its states influencing the others. Italy, Flanders and France were particularly important in this respect and we will look at them in more detail.

Italy

Lace was made in many parts of Italy, but the most important commercial centres were Venice, Genoa, Milan and Burano.

The laces of Venice are famous, which is hardly surprising for during the Renaissance Venice was the most important centre for lovers of all things artistic, luxurious and beautiful. For 200 years she was renowned for her costly silks and her exquisite point and bobbin laces. The Venetians themselves were great hoarders. They regarded the acquisition of wealth as a virtue, and accumulated tremendous riches: jewels, silver, gold, silk and, not least, lace.

One of the earliest laces of Italy, apart from *Reticella*, was a simple twisted and plaited gold lace embroidered with silk. The lace was made of gold thread manufactured from drawn wire or pure gold mixed with laton (a brass-like metal). Silver lace was made in a similar way. Genoa made gold thread as early as the fourteenth century, copying the ancient 'Cyprus Gold'. Venice and Milan also made gold thread, but they began much later than Genoa. Milan was the last place to give up making gold thread in the seventeenth century. (The industry was forced out of existence by heavy taxes.)

Venice

The Venetians were great traders, sailing their galleys around the warm blue Mediterranean and Adriatic seas and farther afield to the cold, grey shores of the British Isles. They brought with them their silver and gold threads, their metal and point laces as well as many other sought-after luxuries such as Malmseys, Muscats and other wines, sweet oils and spices. More important were the new ideas which they spread throughout Europe. The English, with good cause, regarded these wily Venetian merchants with suspicion, and many were the complaints made about the 'cheating Venetians' and their far from honest methods of trading. Inferior thread was habitually sold camouflaged by good thread and, more often than not, it was short in weight.

England had previously purchased her gold thread from Cyprus, but in the sixteenth century the Turks put a stop to all English trade in the Mediterranean, leaving the rascally Venetians with a ready market for their expensive 'Venice Gold'.

'Fringes of Venice' and 'mantel laces of white silk and Venys Gold' appeared at the coronation of Richard III in 1483. There are a few mentions of 'Venice Gold' and 'Venice Fringes' in the reigns of Henry VII and Henry VIII, but it is not until the reign of Elizabeth I that 'cutworks' and Venice point lace came into general use in England. At the same time France also started importing Venice points. By 1626 they were widely used in Europe and England. France, in particular, imported vast quantities.

Sumptuary laws regulating private expenditure in the State's interest were passed in many countries with the object of restricting the import of foreign point laces, but lace continued to flow into them virtually unchecked. The sumptuary laws did at times, however, profoundly affect the lace-making industries of certain countries.

Such laws were designed to curb extravagance in dress. One of the first of these was passed in France as early as the year 608, and many followed during the next 1,000 years or so throughout the whole of Europe. They were even applied to the early settlers in America. Many of them now seem ludicrous. Philip Augustus of France (1179–1223) decreed that no lady, unless she was a lady of the manor, could have more than two dresses a year. No burgess was allowed to spend more

than six francs a yard on any material, but a lady of superior rank might spend up to eight francs a yard. No burgess was allowed to own a carriage, nor was he allowed to dress in green, grey or ermine. The punishment for breaking this law was to forfeit the forbidden article for one year from Easter to Easter.

England, too, had its sumptuary laws. Henry VIII passed various 'Actes of Apparell' in 1509, and another, five years later, was 'agaynst wearing of costly apparell'. Anyone below the rank of knight was forbidden to wear clothing trimmed with lace. Elizabeth I followed in her father's footsteps and passed similar laws during her reign.

In France and England there was a healthy disregard for the laws, and they were obeyed only half-heartedly. In Venice, however, the sumptuary laws had to be taken seriously because citizens were liable to severe punishment if they disobeyed them. The Venetians in the fifteenth and sixteenth centuries were the leaders of court fashion in Europe. They were very jealous of their position and, as a result, their sumptuary laws were the most strict and complicated in Europe. One, issued by the Venetian State in 1542, forbade any citizen to wear metal lace more than 5cm (2in.) wide in case he should injure himself on it.

Not all sumptuary laws were as absurd as this, and many were introduced for sound reasons. They were designed, however, to keep a person firmly in the social class into which he had been born. No one was allowed to ape his betters in matters of dress. Rules were even laid down as to the type of clothing a slave could wear. They were also designed to prevent people of all classes from ruining themselves financially by spending vast sums on clothes they could not afford. A Genoese law of 1449 illustrates this point. It stated that excesses in dress, particularly among women, were not only displeasing to God but brought ruin and destruction to banks. These excesses caused many banks to go into liquidation and draw up illicit contracts. To dress more moderately would release large sums of money, kept unproductive in clothes and jewels, for business purposes which, in turn, could bring great profits.

Clothes and jewels were often used as currency in fifteenth-century Genoa, and vast sums of money were invested in rich clothing. The Martelli family of Florence had clothing to the equivalent value of several houses. It would be interesting to compare the value of our clothing today against the value of our houses.

Sumptuary laws often did considerable harm to the luxury trades, particularly that of lace making, for they not only prevented people from wearing foreign lace but also home-produced lace.

France solved its importation problems when Jean Colbert, Minister of Interior to Louis XIV, established the *Point de France* lace industry near Alençon in 1665. This hit the Venice workers badly because France was a big consumer of Venice points. Not only did France stop importing Venetian lace, it also exported large quantities of its own lace to England, which had also been a customer of the Venetians. In 1680 it was said that much of the lace that was called *Point de Venice* actually came from France.

Until the end of the eighteenth century the Venetians were content to wear their own laces, but after that fashions changed, and their fancy began to stray towards the lighter, more delicate foreign laces. In 1770, at the marriage of the Doge's son, the altar was decorated in Venice point, but the bride and all her attendants were charmingly arrayed in exquisite tuckers and sleeve falls of the finest Brussels lace.

Both point and bobbin lace was made in Venice from the fifteenth century, but they were at their best during the sixteenth and seventeenth centuries. Although some very beautiful bobbin lace was made in Venice, it was eclipsed by the superb needlepoint laces.

The principal needlepoint laces of Venice were **Venice Point** or **Flat Point** (*Point de Venise* or *Point Plat*), **Corraline Point**, **Rose** (Raised) **Point**, **Gros Point**, and **Grounded Venice Point** (*Point de Venise à Réseau*). All of them except the Grounded Venice Point were guipure laces.

Venice Point, a flat needlepoint lace, came first. An early variety of this was corraline point. The lace has a romantic little story attached to it. A girl who made point lace had a sailor sweetheart. Once when he sailed home from some distant ocean he brought her a bunch of corraline. (Corraline is a seaweed which has become encrusted with lime which gives it a graceful white structure, and is also known as 'mermaid's lace'.) The girl was so enchanted by her gift that she copied it in a lace design, and the irregular, almost patternless, guipure now called corraline lace was the result.

Following the Venice Point came the Rose (Raised) Point and the *Gros Point*. These padded laces were made initially as a novelty but Venice Point became the most famous and sought after lace that Venice ever made. It was worn on all full dress and state occasions throughout Europe in the seventeenth and eighteenth centuries.

Grounded Venice Point (*Point de Venise à Réseau*) came later in the seventeenth century. This was so similar to Alençon Point that it is debatable as to which lace was made first. Possibly the Venetians were attempting to win back the trade lost to the *Point de France* industry by copying the French lace. On the other hand, the Alençon Point could equally have been a copy of the Venetian lace. The Venetian lace was, however, superior to that of the early Alençon. Unfortunately, its very delicacy was its downfall because it could not stand up to wear and tear and very little of it exists today, except for a few specimens in museums and private collections. The early Venetian points had very stiff and formal patterns, but with the Renaissance more graceful, flowing designs appeared.

In the late nineteenth century when machine-made lace was plentiful, a polychrome lace was made in Venice. It was a bobbin lace of many colours with designs of fruit, flowers or animals.

Burano

As the island of Burano is so near to Venice it is surprising that its lace did not bear a greater resemblance to that of Venice guipure points. In fact, the old **Burano Point** had a mesh ground similar to that of the Grounded Venice Point. It was, however, coarser and stronger, and as a result more of it survived. Burano Point also resembled Alençon Point, and some of the later Alençon patterns were copied by the Burano workers. The Burano lace-making industry also survived much longer than that of Venice and was still producing lace in the early nineteenth century. It completely died out in the 1860s only to undergo a remarkable revival in 1872 as an antidote to the poverty, distress and semi-starvation afflicting the area at that time.

In 1872 the winter in the Venice region was so severe that all the lakes and lagoons were frozen solid for many months. Fishing, the main livelihood of the area, was impossible and the population was on the brink of starvation. A distress fund was set up, and contributions flooded in. Once the immediate distress was relieved, it was decided to set up a local industry for making fishing nets where women could work if a similar calamity befell their menfolk again. The industry soon failed because the fishermen were too poor to buy the nets.

A certain Signor Fambri suggested that an attempt should be made to revive the old lace industry, and some titled ladies were asked to establish a lace-making school, for by this time the art had virtually died out. Eventually one very old lady was found who still remembered the art of making Burano Point. However, as she was too old to teach in a school, she taught a younger, intelligent and capable woman how to make the local lace. The latter, in turn, taught the first eight pupils at the New Burano School of Lace. These first pupils were paid by the day to persuade them to attend. By the end of the century there were over 400 workers making lace as a livelihood. The young men of the area, with an eye to financial security, eagerly sought lace makers for wives.

Once thoroughly established, the Burano school made not only Burano Point, but also many other beautiful laces in-cluding *Point d'Alençon, Point de Gazé, Point d'Angleterre, Point d'Argentan* and the Venetian points. The girls were very well taught by professional designers from abroad. (In the nineteenth century, however, workers from Alençon were teaching Italians the skills that the Venetians had taught the French in the seventeenth century!)

Genoa

As we have seen, Genoa was one of the first places in Italy to imitate the gold thread and gold laces of Cyprus. At one time Genoa also produced both needlepoint and bobbin lace, but little is heard of the needlepoint because the bobbin lace out-shone it. The lace known as **Genoa Point** (*Point de Gennes*) was all bobbin-made lace. As Venice was the centre for needlepoint lace, so Genoa became the centre of bobbin lace in the sixteenth and seventeenth centuries.

The first we hear in England of lace from Genoa is a mention in the Great Wardrobe Accounts of Elizabeth I, but the laces mentioned were all of silk. The points of Genoa were not in general use throughout Europe until the seventeenth century, when the Genoa industry was at its best. Genoese lace was not usually sold by the yard, but was made into articles such as handkerchiefs, collars and aprons.

The Genoese did not wear lace themselves until the seventeenth century. A visitor to Genoa in 1589 commented: 'The Genoese wear no lace or gardes' (lace trimmings). Another traveller in Italy eight years later noticed with great surprise that the Genoese did not even wear Flemish lace, let alone their own. By the mid-seventeenth century, the Genoese were catching up with current fashions in lace-crazy Europe, for at last they were wearing their own beautiful point laces. Even the peasant women sported aprons and head-dresses trimmed with home-made lace. The Genoese sumptuary laws prohibited the wearing of gold and silver lace within the city walls and the most ornate dresses ever allowed to the women were those of black velvet trimmed with home-produced lace.

Towards the end of the eighteenth century import restrictions imposed by other countries, particularly France, caused an inevitable decline in the Genoese lace industry and the Genoese made lace for home consumption only. In the middle of the nineteenth century, however, Genoa began to produce guipure lace again especially for export to France. Lace making was not confined to the city of Genoa itself but extended east and west along the Italian Riviera. The lace workers were chiefly the wives and daughters of the coral fishermen who supported themselves by lace making when their men were at sea.

In the church of Santa Margherita, a town to the east of Genoa, an old accounts book lists gifts of coral nets given by local fishermen, and bobbin lace given by their womenfolk in 1592. These gifts were thank offerings for the safe return of the men from a long and perilous journey at sea. Old parchment patterns from around the same date and found in the same church were for a tape guipure lace. This confirms that lace was made in the area from a very early date. Much tape guipure was exported to America.

Later, when the demand for point lace had declined, the area went over to making black blonde lace in imitation of Chantilly. In the nineteenth century the centres for blonde lace were Genoa and Cantu, a town near Lake Como.

When machine-made net appeared, Genoa, like Honiton and Brussels, made use of this and embroidered it with flowers and sprigs.

Genoa also had links with macramé work (macramé is an Arabic word meaning 'fringe for trimming'). Macramé work was taught in schools and convents along the Italian Riviera to children of all ages and both sexes. It was mostly used for decorating towels. When the towels were made, long fringes were left at either end, which were then knotted together. A great deal of this macramé work was exported to both North and South America, and some very elaborate designs were exhibited in the Paris Exhibition of 1867. The macramé industry was another way of competing with machines.

Milan

This is one of the oldest lace-making centres in Italy. Its earliest laces were *Reticella* and the silk and gold laces already mentioned, but, as we have seen from the Sforza family inventory, needlepoint and bobbin lace was made in Milan as early as the fifteenth century.

After this document there is very little mention in Italy of early Milanese lace. In England Henry VIII bought a pair of hose for his ample legs, edged with purple silk and gold lace from Milan. In 1606, James I, who was not renowned for his fashion sense, purchased 'one suit, with cannons there unto, of silk lace shadowed with silk Milan lace'. In the same year James's queen bought for her new baby 'lace, Milan fashion for a child's waistcoat'.

Like Genoa, the well known Milan points were all bobbin laces and were at their best in the seventeenth century. Lace was vital to the economy of Milan, which also eventually fell victim of the import laws and changes in fashion.

France

During the sixteenth and early seventeenth centuries French laces were much inferior to those of neighbouring Italy and Flanders. The discerning French buyers realised this, and vast quantities of foreign lace poured into France. As a result, large sums of money flowed out of the country to the detriment of the French economy. Many sumptuary laws were passed forbidding the French to wear foreign lace, but to no avail. The French could not be persuaded to give up exquisite foreign points for the coarser laces of home manufacture.

In 1660 a law of Louis XIV forbade the wearing of foreign lace, and even French lace which was wider than 2.5cm (1in.). A little concession was made by allowing all those who possessed a collarette or manchette (wrist ruffle) to wear them for one year after which, it was hoped, they would be worn out. Jean Colbert, among others, realized that such a law could not be enforced, and devised a scheme whereby France could make its own point lace and be independent of foreign-made products. He encouraged a number of skilled Venetian lace makers to settle in France and train the French in Venetian methods. At first the French workers found the new lace making techniques much more demanding, and preferred to make the simpler coarse laces they were used to. Eventually, however, Colbert's plan succeeded, and in 1665 the manufacture of **Point de France** was established. At first, the lace was almost identical to the Venetian point laces, but as the French workers became more skilled, the style changed. The lace became lighter and more delicate, and its name was changed to **Point d'Alençon**. *Point d'Alençon* was perhaps the finest lace ever to be made in France, and eventually it surpassed the point laces of Italy.

Venice was incensed by losing so many of its finest lace makers to France, and issued the following decree against the offending workers and their families:

> If any artist or handicraftsman practises his art in any foreign land to the detriment of the Venetian Republic, order to return will be sent him; if he disobeys then, his nearest of kin will be put into prison, in order that through his interest in their welfare his obedience may be compelled. If he comes back his past offence will be condoned, and employment for him will be found in Venice, but if, notwithstanding the imprisonment of his nearest of kin, he obstinately decides to continue living abroad, an emissary will be commissioned to kill him, and his next of kin will only be liberated upon his death.

The Venetians were not alone in their anger. Flanders, alarmed at the numbers of Flemish workers who emigrated to France, also passed an Act in Brussels, in 1698, threatening to punish anyone who enticed away its workers.

The *Point de France* when first produced was so expensive that only the very rich could afford it. The less wealthy had to be content with the cheaper bobbin laces, and the demand for these grew rapidly, thus causing a swift expansion of the French bobbin lace industry. The demand became so great that the lace towns could not attract enough workers to meet it, and much of the French bobbin lace was made by cottagers who worked at home.

In the nineteenth century, *Point d'Alençon* was also made in Burano, Brussels and Bayeux.

Chantilly

Chantilly, situated near Paris, became famous for its black silk lace, much worn in the eighteenth century by French royalty, particularly the unlucky Marie Antoinette, wife of Louis XVI. The French Revolution temporarily closed the Chantilly lace industry when the blood-thirsty revolutionaries sent many of the lace makers to the guillotine along with their royal patrons.

Napoleon revived the Chantilly industry and once again it became prosperous. The Chantilly lace workers made both the white blonde lace which was high fashion in Paris at the beginning of the seventeenth century, and the traditional black lace which was exported to Spain and the Spanish American colonies where it was highly prized for mantillas and scarves.

Chantilly thrived because it was so close to Paris, the centre of fashion; it ultimately declined for the same reason. Towards the end of the nineteenth century new industries opened in the French capital, and the Chantilly lace makers left the industry for the higher wages offered elsewhere. After the Chantilly industry faded, the lace was still made in several towns in Normandy; indeed, many of the famous 'Chantilly' shawls were in fact made in Bayeux.

Lille

Lille was not only important in French lace making history, it also greatly influenced English lace manufacture, particularly in the Midland counties, as many of Lille workers fled to England to escape religious persecution. Lille ground was used in Buckinghamshire lace.

Lace making in Lille dates back to the sixteenth century. Lille, once a Flemish town, was handed over to France in 1668 by treaty. As a result many Lille workers moved to Ghent, a town which was still Flemish. This deprived Lille of many of its best workers but, in spite of this, its lace industry still thrived, and continued to make both black and white laces. Wide black Lille lace was very popular in the eighteenth century for trimming the fashionable long silk mantles (cloaks). The English, in particular, adored Lille lace, and enormous quantities were smuggled into England; 1789 was a peak year for smuggled Lille lace (see Chapter 7).

The prosperity of the Lille industry at its height can be judged by the fact that in 1788 there were more than 16,000 workers in Lille, and the lace produced was worth more than £160,000 – equivalent to several million pounds at today's valuation.

Lille lace was a very light and dainty bobbin lace which in the eighteenth century was extensively referred to as 'Migonettes' and 'Blonde de Fil'.

Arras

Arras, like Lille, was also a Flemish town ceded to France in 1668. Although much better known for its tapestries than its lace, Arras made a lace almost identical to that of Lille, except that it was slightly coarser.

Valenciennes

Valenciennes was also a Flemish town which became French in 1678. It is claimed that lace was made in Valenciennes as early as the fifteenth century, but there is no real evidence to substantiate this. Valenciennes lace probably dates from the introduction of the Colbert lace industries. The Valenciennes industry was at its peak from 1725 to 1780; it then declined. The decline was partly due to a change in fashion and partly due to the very high cost of the lace. A skilled worker could make only about 4cm (approximately 1½in.) a day, and it often took a whole year to make 60cm (24in.). By comparison, a Lille worker could make 270 to 360cm (3 to 4 yards) a day. Valenciennes was popularly used for making men's ruffles and ladies' caps. Ruffle lace cost around nine guineas (£9.45) for an ell (about 120cm, 4ft), which was highly expensive, and it took about an ell to make a pair of ruffles. Valenciennes was also used for babies' clothes and underwear because of its hard-wearing qualities. After 1780 ruffles became unfashionable, and the daintier laces of Brussels, Lille and Arras

became popular with the ladies, replacing the costly Valenciennes. The other laces were cheaper because they could be made more quickly.

Valenciennes lace was often called 'les belles eternelles Valenciennes'. It was famous for its durability, and regarded as a family heirloom to be handed down from mother to daughter. Not only the rich coveted the beautiful Valenciennes lace; peasants would save up for many years to buy a piece of *vraie Valenciennes* to make a bonnet or trim a head-dress.

Vraie Valenciennes (real Valenciennes) was so called because it was supposed to be the only lace which was made within the city wall itself; any lace made in the surrounding neighbourhood was termed *fausse Valenciennes* (false Valenciennes). It was claimed that if a piece of lace was started in the city and finished outside, the differences between the two parts could be distinctly seen. It was also claimed that if two people worked on the same piece of lace the different workmanship could be detected. This was often used as a selling gimmick, for the lace fetched a higher price if it could be said that it was 'made by the same hand'.

Young girls were always employed to make Valenciennes because their hands were soft, smooth and uncalloused and their eyesight was usually much keener. These young girls worked in underground cellars because the damp air was better for the ultra fine flax thread used for the lace. As a result of these working conditions the girls' eyesight deteriorated rapidly, and by the time they were 30 many were almost blind. They were also prey to rheumatism, arthritis and chest complaints through leaning over their lace pillows in damp conditions for many hours a day without respite.

By 1790 the Valenciennes industry had almost disappeared, and in spite of Napoleon's efforts to revive it, it had vanished by the mid-nineteenth century. Valenciennes lace, however, was made in other towns such as Le Puy, the oldest lace making centre in France.

French laces were also made in many other districts including Normandy, which was famous for its blonde laces.

Flanders

The Flemish were the first to perfect the art of making bobbin lace, and the industry became a great source of wealth to Flanders. It was the mainstay of the country even during the religious persecutions of the sixteenth century when so many skilled workers fled from Flanders to take refuge in more tolerant lands such as England, Germany and America. England owes the bobbin lace of the East Midland counties to Lille and Mechlin, and the laces of Devon to the influence of Brussels workers.

The whole Flemish economy was at times solely dependent on lace making. By a royal command of Charles V (1519–1556) all girls from the age of five were taught the art of lace making in schools and convents. Vast quantities of lace were exported. In 1768 Flanders exported so much lace to England that the difference between England's imports and exports of lace was £250,000, a considerable sum in those days.

The earliest lace believed to have been made in Flanders was a tape lace, sometimes called **Pillow Guipure**. The braid was joined either by bars or fastened together where the braid touched.

One of the earliest Flemish laces was **Trolle Kant** – *kant* being the Flemish for lace. It was a bobbin lace, sometimes of very beautiful design, and was made in the sixteenth, seventeenth and eighteenth centuries. English 'trolly' lace takes its name from this Flemish term. It was a coarse lace with a thick cordonnet and grounds like the old Flemish grounds. Trolly lace was also made in Normandy. All the very early Flemish laces required large numbers of bobbins and had very intricate patterns. Eventually each town in Flanders developed its own design, but until the eighteenth century all designs tended to resemble each other.

Brussels

Brussels lace was either needlepoint (*point d'aiguille*) or bobbin (*point plat*). The early needlepoint lace was known as **Point de Bruxelles**, but in the nineteenth century it developed into **Point de Gaze**. The very old bobbin lace was made in one piece on the pillow, flowers and the ground together. Very little of this old bobbin lace or of the *Point de Bruxelles* exists today and what there is is in museums. All other Brussels lace was made in motif form. The motifs (sprigs) were made separately with the needle or bobbins, and either sewn into the ground or linked in with bobbins. The ground of the Brussels lace was also made either with the needle or with bobbins, but it is the extreme fineness of the flax thread used which makes it such a distinctive and lovely lace.

A Scottish nobleman who visited Brussels in the late eighteenth century had nursed the idea that he could introduce the art of making Brussels lace into his own Scottish parish. He was soon disillusioned. He brought a friend a present, and wrote:

> This day I bought you some ruffles and some beautiful Brussels lace, the most light and costly of all manufactures – The thread is of the most exquisite fineness that they cannot make it in this country. Five or six different artists are employed to form the nice part of this fabric so that it is a complicated art which cannot be transplanted. . . . At Brussels, from one pound of flax alone they can manufacture to the value of £700 sterling.

The flax thread from which Brussels lace was made had one great fault: it discoloured very quickly. Water, air, heat or just general use made the thread turn from white to its natural cream colour. The lace makers tried various chemicals, even white lead, to prevent discolouration, but none was effective. During the eighteenth century the lace was powdered to keep it white, but eventually the natural cream-coloured Brussels lace became fashionable. It was then dipped into coffee to deepen the hue. This light coffee colour was known as 'Isabelle' tint.

The needlepoint ground in Brussels lace was about three times as expensive to make as the bobbin ground. The bobbin ground (*droschel* ground) was made in strips of about 2.5cm (1in.) wide, and joined together with a needle and a special stitch called *point raccroc* (fine joining). *Point de Gazé* was one of the lightest of Brussels laces because the needle ground was a net made by a single looped stitch with no twists. Another type of Brussels lace was called **Brussels Rose Point**. Extra petals were added to the needlepoint flowers making them three-dimensional. This lace was made towards the end of the nineteenth century. Yet another type was guipure lace in which the motifs were joined by bars.

One of the most interesting and controversial laces to come from Brussels was **English Point** (*Point d'Angleterre*). With such a name one naturally assumes that this lace must have been English, and indeed some authorities do still claim that it was made in England, especially as it resembles Honiton Lace in some respects. The theory as to the origin of English point, which is now generally accepted as being correct, is that it was made in Brussels, smuggled into England, and then sold as English Point to avoid heavy customs duty.

In 1662, during the reign of Charles II, an Act was passed forbidding the wearing of foreign laces, although there was a heavy demand for Brussels lace at court. The English lace merchants, who faced heavy financial losses as a result of this Act, evolved a plan whereby Flemish lace workers were to be encouraged to settle in England to make Brussels lace for the court. The scheme had to be abandoned because it was impossible to obtain the fine flax thread. After this failure Brussels lace was smuggled into England by the merchants who sold it as *Point d'Angleterre* (**English Point**). As a result, from the end of the seventeenth century Brussels lace was known as *Point d'Angleterre*.

Lace where the motifs were connected with bars was called **Point d'Angleterre a Brides**. *Point d'Angleterre* was one of the most exquisite laces ever made, but in spite of this it must have been boring and unrewarding to make, for it was manufactured on a production-line basis. One girl made the ground; a second made the footing; a third made the flowers; a fourth made the openwork centre to the flowers; a

fifth joined the strips of bobbin ground; and yet another joined the various components together. The last girl must have been the only one who could really feel any sense of achievement, for she alone, apart from the designer, saw the finished article. The designer, or master, was responsible for the initial design, choosing the thread, pricking the parchment, dividing it into various sections, and allocating them to different workers.

Brussels lace retained its popularity because it changed in style to accommodate the fashions of the day. The designs ranged from the old formal Gothic patterns, through the flowing lines of the Renaissance, to modern informal flower sprigs and sprays. When machine-made bobbin net arrived, Brussels adapted itself once again, and both needle-made and bobbin-made motifs were appliquéed on to the net. Quite often the needlepoint and bobbin sprays were mixed. In fact, in most Brussels bobbin lace there is a small portion of needlepoint somewhere. Sprigs and flower sprays were sold separately. In the nineteenth century another Flemish town, Binche, made many of the flowers for the appliqué work.

Mechlin

With the exception of Brussels lace, all Flemish laces were known until 1665 in the French commercial world as *Malines*. The lace we now know as **Mechlin** was unknown before 1630. In England Mechlin was also known as 'Macklin'.

Mechlin is a light dainty lace which became very popular in England at the end of the seventeenth century. It was a favourite lace of Queen Anne, Queen Charlotte, and also of Napoleon, who once likened it to the tracery of the spires of Antwerp Cathedral.

English Buckinghamshire lace is based on Mechlin patterns with Lille grounds, but some of the early Bedfordshire and Buckinghamshire laces were entirely Mechlin designs.

Binche

Binche was a town in the old Flemish province of Hainault. Its lace industry began in the early 1600s, and a great deal of lace was made in the seventeenth and eighteenth centuries. Most of the lace was made in the convents and the income it generated helped to maintain them.

The lace produced was called **Guipure de Binche**, a bobbin lace with a complex ground of rosettes and spiders which closely resembled old Valenciennes lace. This likeness to Valenciennes is attributed to the fact that the town of Valenciennes, before becoming French in 1678, also belonged to the old province of Hainault.

One picturesque account of the Binche lace industry described Binche as 'a hive of lace makers and the bees of this hive earned so much money by making lace that their husbands could go and take a walk without care for the morrow.'* Unfortunately the 'hive' ran out of honey, for the production of hand-made lace declined when machine-made lace arrived, after which Binche concentrated on making sprigs for appliqué onto the machine-made net for Brussels lace. **Guipure de Binche** is now called by the modern name of *Point de Fee*. It is still made today, but it is very expensive.

Flemish lace was also made in Bruges and Antwerp. Early lace made in Bruges was called **Guipure de Flandres**. In the nineteenth century 'duchess' lace was made, so called because it was named after the Duchess of Brabant.

---

* Mrs Bury Palliser, *History of Lace*, 4th ed., 1902

3 Early Lace
in Other Countries

Spain

Spain has been making lace since medieval times. Her early laces were drawnwork, cutwork and darned netting as well as gold and silver lace. She did not make either needlepoint or bobbin lace until it had been established in Italy, France and Flanders. Traditionally, it is said that Italy taught Spain how to make needlepoint lace and Flanders taught her the art of bobbin lace. This is quite likely, since Flanders was a dominion of Spain in the sixteenth century and Spain imported many luxury goods from Flanders, including a great deal of lace and linen. It would have been simple and natural for Spain to have copied the Flemish laces.

The famous Spanish point (*point d'Espagne*) of the sixteenth and seventeenth centuries was not a thread lace, however, but lace of gold and silver, sometimes embroidered with coloured silks.

In the fifteenth century the making of gold Spanish point was largely controlled by the Spanish Jews, but towards the end of the fifteenth century, in 1492, all the Jews were expelled from Spain. As a result the production of gold lace deteriorated rapidly and the Spanish Grandees, who had been prolific buyers of gold lace and refused to be deprived of it, turned to the much better products of Italy. In 1494 the imports of gold lace from Lucca and Florence were banned by law and only those to be used exclusively for church purposes were allowed into Spain.

The gold Spanish point reached its peak in the seventeenth century. France, in particular, bought large quantities of it in the mid-seventeenth century during the early years of the reign of Louis XIV.

There is a school of thought, however, which contends that in the sixteenth and seventeenth centuries much of the so called 'Spanish point' was in fact made in France and Italy, and that it was only called 'Spanish' because of the large amounts used by the Spanish Grandees. Whatever the facts are, the Spanish Grandees presumably found ways and means of getting round the import restrictions, or else Spain produced sufficient for home consumption in the sixteenth century.

The other lace known as 'Spanish point' (*Point d'Espagne*) is a beautiful, heavy needlepoint lace. Large quantities of this lace came to light in 1830 when the Spanish monasteries were closed and a surprised world found that they contained a great deal of the most exquisite lace. Much of the newly discovered lace was either of Italian origin or had been copied from Venice points. A lot of Italian lace must have been imported into Spain for church use and the designs copied by the nuns over the centuries. So the claim that Italy taught Spain how to make point lace could be justified. Many of the nuns were natives of other countries who had obviously taken their own lace with them. One piece of lace, found unfinished, was some *Point d'Alençon*.

The religious establishments in Spain produced most of the thread lace and it was made primarily for the use of the church. The images of the Madonna and patron saints were dressed every day in fresh sets of lace-trimmed robes. In major churches the figures were dressed and re-dressed two or three times a day. The value of the robes in such churches was so great that a Mistress of the Robes of the Madonna was appointed to care for them.

In 1623 Philip III of Spain passed a sumptuary law curtailing the use of lace and other finery, so the Spanish court used it only on occasions when, for example, it deliberately set out to impress visiting royalty. One such occasion took place, in 1623, when Prince Charles of England (the future Charles I) visited Spain in connection with his proposed marriage to the Spanish Infanta which, of course, never took place.

During this visit the sumptuary law was suspended and the Queen of Spain even sent Prince Charles ten trunks filled with linen, heavily trimmed with lace. The Queen, it seems, believed that Charles had not been well provided for in the matter of lace. According to the records of the 'Extraordinary Expenses of his Highness to Spain 1623' however, quite a lot of money had been expended on lace-trimmed ruffs, cuffs and hats, not to mention 30 lace-trimmed shirts for the eight footmen travelling with Prince Charles.

Spain also made black and white blonde laces which were largely used for mantillas. Silk for these laces was produced near Barcelona and much of the lace was also made there or in Catalonia. Spanish blonde had a light net background which resembled Lille ground, with very heavy, closely worked designs. The Spanish blonde never equalled those of Chantilly, Bayeux or Caen. The patterns were often irregular, and the reason for this, perhaps, was that the peasants worked in their own homes and there was very little central control over the standard of the work. The Spanish lady was lucky – her Mantilla was considered sacred and could never be confiscated for debt.

Holland

Although very little is known about early Dutch lace, by the seventeenth century Holland was exporting lace to Spain, Portugal and even to Italy. When Colbert set up the lace industry in France the French tried to infiltrate the Dutch markets, but the Dutch managed to hold their own even though the competition was very strong, and they even succeeded in exporting some of their lace into France itself.

The Dutch lace industry was given a boost in 1685 when 4,000 Huguenot workers from the Alençon region of France fled to Holland, and set up a lace industry in Amsterdam. Later another Huguenot refugee introduced gold and silver laces into Holland.

Even though Holland was more fortunate than the other lace-making countries of Europe in having the unique flax thread produced in Haarlem, Dutch needlepoint laces never became famous like those of Flanders. In the eighteenth century most Dutch laces were made for home consumption only, and any small surpluses usually went to Italy. Dutch lace was imported into England only occasionally. The Dutch themselves were great users of lace, especially in their homes; brasses and bed pans were shrouded in good point lace, and the arrival of a baby was proudly proclaimed by adding a lace wrapping to the door knocker of the new parents' home.

Eighteenth-century Dutch bobbin lace was very firm, thick and durable. In some respects it resembled Valenciennes in that it incorporated natural flower patterns and leaves in its designs, but it was much more suitable for furnishings than for decorating dainty underwear or outer garments.

Germany

Barbara Uttman is buried in a shady churchyard in the Harz mountains of Germany. Over her grave is a tombstone which bears the inscription, 'Here lies Barbara Uttman, died 14 January, 1575 whose invention of lace in the year 1561 made her the benefactress of the Erzgebirge'.

Barbara Uttman did not invent lace, but she did introduce it into Germany. Having learnt lace making herself from a Protestant refugee from Brabant, she then taught the local women and girls how to make lace.

Barbara's father was a burgher with mining interests in the Harz mountains, and Barbara married a rich master miner. The women of the area traditionally made a type of netting for their menfolk to wear over their hair when down the mines. Barbara Uttman taught them how to extend these netting skills to make a plain type of bobbin lace. Later, in 1561, she set up a workshop to make patterned lace. This enterprise expanded rapidly and eventually more than 30,000 were employed in the local lace-making industry. When she died, Barbara Uttman left 65 descendants, children and grandchildren. The number equalled the number of stitches on her first piece of lace, just as a fortune-teller had predicted in the early days of her marriage.

In the eighteenth century a fine lace called **Dresden** was produced in Germany. It became so popular that prizes were offered in both Scotland and Ireland for the best imitation of Dresden work. It was not strictly a lace, but very fine drawn muslin thread work. It was popular for ruffles. Later a Maltese type of bobbin lace was made in Dresden.

Germany, like Holland, benefited from the influx of skilled refugees who fled from France in 1685. The new workers, nicknamed 'haricot bean eaters', made a considerable impact upon Germany's lace industry, particularly in Berlin, Hamburg, Potsdam, Leipzig and Hanover. Lord Nelson purchased some magnificent lace trimming in Hamburg for Lady Nelson, and a black lace cloak for one of his wife's friends.

Germany produced both needlepoint and bobbin lace. At one time Saxony point was an imitation of Brussels lace. Other German laces were developments of *Alençon* as a result of the influence of the French refugees. In the nineteenth century a coarse Torchon lace was made; it was very strong and thick, and acquired the name **Eternal**.

Malta

Malta is a comparative newcomer to lace making, which was introduced on the island by Lady Hamilton Chichester in 1833. Maltese lace is a guipure lace with a distinct Genoese influence. Workers from Genoa went to Malta to teach the Maltese lace making. Both black and white blonde laces were made on the island. The silk for the black blonde lace came from Barcelona, and was similar to that used by the Spanish for their mantillas. A distinguish-

ing feature of Maltese lace is the Maltese cross incorporated in the design.

Scandinavia

Denmark

Cutwork was a speciality of Denmark long before either point or bobbin lace was made in that country. Beautiful cutwork and embroidery decorated all the best Danish table and bed linen, most of which was used only on special family occasions such as marriages, christenings and funerals.

Bobbin lace was introduced into Denmark from Brabant but it was never made on a commercial scale except in the Schleswig region. An industry was set up there in the sixteenth century.

Tönder is the most famous of the Danish laces. In the seventeenth century, in an attempt to improve his country's lace trade, a Danish merchant introduced 12 lace makers from the Dortmund region of Germany to Tönder. These 12 elderly gentlemen, with their long silver beards encased in cloth bags to prevent entanglement with the bobbins, taught the local people to make lace, and soon a thriving industry was established.

Tönder lace was marketed by pedlars known as 'lace postmen'. They travelled on foot throughout Scandinavia and to parts of Germany carrying the lace in leather bags. One lace postman did well enough to buy himself a horse. He estimated that, by the time he had reached retirement, he had travelled the equivalent of three times round the earth.

The early *Tönder* laces had very attractive Flemish grounds. They were so strong and durable that they were regarded as family heirlooms. Dutch flower and various trolly grounds were used. The Flemish patterns died out and were replaced by Mechlin grounds with the patterns run in with coarse thread. Later still, Lille grounds were used in *Tönder* lace. With the arrival of machine-made lace, the hand-made lace industry virtually died out. Lace schools were closed, and lacemakers, who were earning only threepence or fourpence for a sixteen hour day, could make more money on the land. The small amount of lace still made by hand was peddled by hawkers, but they had no capital and could not afford to stock the good, but expensive lace.

Sweden

According to tradition lace making was introduced into the Convent of Vadstena by St Birgitta after a visit to Italy. But this is merely legend for St Birgitta died in 1335, long before lace making was established in Europe.

However, there is little doubt that lace making in Sweden originated in the convents. In the middle ages the nuns of Vadstena made netting caps, embroidered with gold and silver, and from these progressed to lace making. When the Swedish convents were closed down under Charles XI, most of the nuns left for Poland, but those that stayed were given food and accommodation by the local people, and continued to make lace in secret. But the secret was hard to keep, and the art of lace making spread. Today, Vadstena is once again the centre of lace making in Sweden.

Russia

Lace made in Russia dates back only to the nineteenth century. Bright colours were worked into the designs, red and blue being popular. Russian designs were symmetrical and snake-like, sometimes with Torchon or honeycomb grounds. They were probably influenced by the German Torchon laces from Saxony. At the turn of the century a brightly-coloured Torchon-type lace was made at Vologda.

Before the 1917 revolution, Russia imported laces from Europe. When the Russian nobles fled during the revolution they stitched their jewels into undergarments decorated with European lace. The lace from these garments is now on sale in the more exclusive Belgian antique shops at a very high price.

America

Lace making, did not, as many people suppose, just drift into America with the European settlers of the nineteenth century. Lace making was, in fact, introduced into New England from the East Midland counties as early as the seventeenth century. This has been established from the type of lace made and the antique bobbins which have survived.

From various paintings, letters and diaries still in existence, we know that the early American settlers took a certain amount of lace-trimmed clothing with them, in keeping with the fashion of the times. It was worn only on special occasions partly because of the sumptuary laws (one man was punished in 1652 for excess in 'bootes, ribands and silver laces'), and partly because such clothing had to be treasured because it was very difficult to replace in the New World.

These new Americans had been familiar with both needlepoint and bobbin lace before they left their old country, and many of them were skilled in the art of making lace. They could, therefore, both make lace and teach others the art. In lace making they followed the fashions of the Old World, although distance always kept them slightly behind the very latest fashions.

Many Protestant refugees from Europe sought asylum in America after the Revocation of the Edict of Nantes in 1685, and lace making spread to many areas of the country. The earliest records of lace

Diagram 1
Plaque celebrating 300 years of lace making in USA

making on a large scale comes from Ipswich in Massachusetts. Here, both black and white bobbin lace was made with silk and flax thread. By 1790 about 38,000 metres (42,000 yards) were being produced each year. Most of the lace bore a strong resemblance to that of the English Midland counties. In 1930 a plaque was set up in Ipswich, Massachusetts, commemorating 300 years of bobbin lace making in the area. Bobbins, pillows and lace from this era of lace making are still preserved in the museums of Ipswich and in other New England states.

With the invention of machine-made bobbin net, the hand-made bobbin lace industry of Ipswich faded out, and was replaced by the manufacture of **Limerick** lace. Limerick lace was made in America from about 1810 until about 1840, long before it was made in Limerick itself. It was in great demand for veiling to trim the chic poke bonnets fashionable at that time.

Limerick lace making developed into another cottage industry. Housewives spent their mornings doing the chores, and their afternoons making the embroidered Limerick lace.

In the early part of the twentieth century, knitted lace, darned netting, tatting and crochet all had a spell of popularity in America. Now, as in Britain, bobbin lace has been revived as a hobby.

Before leaving America, the lace making of the true natives of that country, the Red Indians, deserves a mention.

With the coming of the white settlers, the Indians' traditional way of life came to an end and, unable to adapt to the new, they sank into abject poverty. This so appalled Sybil Carter, a nineteenth-century missionary, that she decided to help the Indians regain their self respect and to make a living. From their intricate bead and basket work she realized that the Indians were clever with their hands, and she decided to teach them bobbin lace making. In 1890 she went to Italy to learn the art herself. When she returned she established the Sybil Carter Indian Lace Association, and set up eight teaching centres. Six tribes of Indians were represented among her pupils. At first their lack of cleanliness presented great problems, but these were eventually overcome, and the Indians learnt to make very good bobbin lace. Included in the designs were symbols of Indian life such as a squaw with a papoose on her back, Indians hunting duck and Indian tepees, as well as naturalistic flowers, trees and animals. In the early twentieth century this Indian-made lace won a number of gold medals and other awards in international exhibitions.

Canada

Lace making was introduced into Canada 60 years go by an immigrant called Elsie Spencer, who settled on Denman Island off the coast of British Columbia.

Women from the neighbouring islands travelled considerable distances by rowing boats to Denman Island to learn lace making from Elsie Spencer. Initially, many lacked lace making equipment, but resourcefully made their own pillows and bobbins until they could be imported from Britain. Through their enthusiasm lace making gradually spread to the Canadian mainland where it is thriving today in many parts of the country.

4 How Lace came to Britain

England

Although England has never been renowned for its needlepoint lace, nonetheless some very good needlepoint lace was made here during the sixteenth and seventeenth centuries, most of which was *Reticella* cutwork, produced for the home market. In the sixteenth century this lace compared very favourably with French and Italian imports. During that period English needlepoint was made both by professional embroideresses and in homes throughout the country. All classes of English women were taught sewing and embroidery from an early age, and titled ladies sewed as they supervised the maids who stitched the cutwork for the household linen. Some of the early samplers, sewn by small girls, incorporated cutwork stitches.

Needlepoint lace was never produced on an industrial scale in England, and little was made professionally after 1630. It did, however, continue to be made in English homes throughout the seventeenth and eighteenth centuries, and there are a number of pieces of domestic linen still in existence decorated with English cutwork. Although most needlepoint was cutwork, some was worked on a skeleton pattern on parchment.

Hollie Point is the best known of English needlepoint laces. Although mentioned in the seventeenth century, most of it was made during the second half of the eighteenth century. It was mainly used for baby wear, especially to provide ventilated panels on the backs of babies' bonnets and caps, and on the bodices and shoulders of gowns. Although far daintier than any previous English needlepoint, it was also hard wearing.

The art of bobbin lace making was probably introduced into England by Protestant refugees who fled from the Spanish-dominated Low Countries after the re-introduction of the Inquisition by Philip II. More than 100,000 fled to the safety of England, the first of them arriving here in 1563. Among their numbers were a great many skilled lace makers. Some of these refugees settled in the villages of Kent and Sussex while others drifted further north to London. Others, particularly those from the Mechlin area, made their way to small villages in Bedfordshire, such as Cranfield, probably because two influential English families, who were prepared to help Flemish Protestants, lived in that county.

Many of the refugees brought their lace-making equipment with them: lace parchments, covers for their lace pillows, a few bobbins and pins and some thread, in fact just enough for them to start their trade in a new country. Along with the tools of their trade, the refugees also brought vegetable seeds – carrots, parsnips, turnips, cabbages and celery, many of which were virtually unknown in England at that time. Above all, they brought their lace, which was greatly admired by the English and who were soon learning the art of lace making themselves.

From the villages of Bedfordshire the Flemish lace makers spread to Buckinghamshire, settling at Newport Pagnell, Olney and Buckingham, and on into Northamptonshire. Once lace making had become well established in the east Midland counties it was made not only by women and children, but also by men after spending their working day in the fields. From the east Midlands bobbin lace making spread to parts of Huntingdonshire, Hertfordshire, Oxfordshire, Cambridgeshire and West Suffolk and then on down into the western counties of Hampshire, Wiltshire, Dorset, Somerset and Devon. Later, lace making was mostly confined to Bedfordshire, Buckinghamshire, Northamptonshire, Huntingdonshire and Oxfordshire. In the west, Somerset, Devon and Dorset were the main lace making counties.

Devon's famous **Honiton** lace was first referred to in a document of 1620 by T. Westcot, who wrote *View of Devon*. Even then, he regarded lace making in Devon as an old established industry. That, together with the similarity between the laces of Brussels and Honiton, suggests that the refugees from Flanders brought lace making to Devon. An old tombstone near a wall of old Honiton Church also suggests that lace making was well established in the area in the early seventeenth century. It is inscribed:

Here lyeth ye body of James Rodge, of Honinton, in ye County of Devonshire (Bonelace Siller, hath given unto the poore of Honinton P'ishe, the benyfitt of £100 for ever), who deceased ye 27 of July Aº Dⁱ 1617 AETATAE SVAE 50 Remember the Poore.

Not a great deal is known of Wiltshire lace, but some excellent laces were made in Dorset in the eighteenth century. The main centres were Blandford, Lyme Regis and Sherborne. **Blandford Point** was used for cravats, but only the rich could afford this superb lace for it cost £30 a metre (yard). The industry at Blandford was almost wiped out when the town was devastated by fire in 1731.

After the Massacre of St Bartholomew in France in 1572, another wave of refugees arrived in England. Amongst these French Huguenots there were many lace makers, chiefly from Lille and the surrounding district. They joined forces with the Flemish lace makers who had already settled in the Midlands, and it is interesting to see the influences of both the Lille and the Mechlin workers in the old English laces. Many of these have Mechlin designs worked on a Lille ground, now referred to as Bucks point ground in England.

The influx of Protestant refugees from Europe continued until 1598 when the Edict of Nantes was signed, allowing Protestants freedom of worship. With the revocation of this edict in 1685, already mentioned, refugees again started arriving in England. Many were from Burgundy and Normandy, and again England gained lace makers among them. Most of these found their way to the districts in England where lace making had become an established industry. Local collections were organized for these 'French Protestants', much as we might collect today for victims of natural disasters. In a village near Olney, in Buckinghamshire, an old register has an entry dated 16 February 1686: 'collected for the French Protestants £2. 10s', a generous sum in those days. England was repaid for this hospitality for not only the lace industry but the entire English economy benefited from this influx of highly-skilled workers in many trades.

There are other theories about the introduction of bobbin lace making into Britain. One is that the art was first taught in Bedfordshire by Queen Catherine of Aragon as early as 1531. She stayed in Ampthill in Bedfordshire for a short time while waiting for her divorce from Henry VIII and during that time, it is said, she instructed the villagers in lace making. According to one legend, when the local people could not afford to buy bread, the Queen burnt all her lace so that orders for new would create employment for the poor. To support this theory there is a lace stitch called kat stitch and a pattern known as Queen Catherine's pattern. It seems to be accepted now that the Queen's lace was probably a type of cutwork. However, when Catherine first came to England to marry Prince Arthur, Henry VIII's older brother, in 1501, bobbin lace was not widely established on the Continent, so she was hardly likely to be skilled in making it. Another theory is that bobbin lace making was already carried on in England as a domestic craft and that the Flemish and French refugees merely developed it into an industry.

In spite of these conflicting theories, the earliest references to the art of bobbin lace making in England are connected with the refugees.

Scotland

Little lace was made in Scotland until the mid-eighteenth century when the Duchess of Hamilton, inspired by lace she had seen on the continent, brought over a lace mistress from France and set up a school for spinning and bobbin lace making. The pupils, who were provided with free food and clothing, were 12 seven-year-old girls who were to stay at the school until they reached 14.

The **Hamilton** lace produced by the girls was not very good, being rather coarse with poor designs. Nevertheless, it did cause some influential Scots to take a look at the arts and industries of their country. As a result The Select Society of Edinburgh was formed in 1754 to encourage the arts of Scotland.

The society, concerned by the size of Scotlands imports of bobbin lace and ready-made ruffles, decided to offer two prizes for home-produced lace: one for the best imitation of Dresden work or for a pair of men's ruffles, and the other for 'the best bone lace, not under 20 yards'. Each of the winners was to get five guineas (£5.25) or a gold medal. Since the Duke of Hamilton was the patron of the society, Hamilton lace won many of the prizes even though it had little to recommend it.

During the society's ten-year life span it had stimulated interest in lace making throughout Scottish society. Moreover, lace making had become not only a livelihood for the poor, but also for gentlewomen who had found themselves impoverished after the Jacobite risings of 1745. Whilst the Scots Jacobite Party supported Scotland there were many Scots who supported England and were loyal to the Royal House of Hanover. The latter group was angry at the Scots Jacobites for sending the sum of £400,000 to France in 1763 to support exiled members of their party. In 1764 the *Edinburgh Advertiser* said that these exiles 'learn nothing but folly and extravagances,' which included a taste for foreign lace. As a consequence all foreign lace, but not English, was banned from Scotland. Tremendous efforts were made to improve Scotland's own lace-making industry, and more than £200,000-worth of thread was purchased from Lille each year to be used in Scottish lace production. So keen were the authorities to preserve the quality of Scottish lace that any badly spun thread from Lille was immediately confiscated by the Stamp Master and burnt, so that it could never find its way on to the market by devious means. The burning of Lille thread became a frequent occurence.

Like many other countries Scotland had problems in enforcing its Customs laws, and only a decade after foreign lace had been banned plenty of Brussels and fine point lace was available in Scotland.

By the end of the eighteenth century, Scottish lace making began to decline, and was replaced by tambouring net and by Ayrshire (Scotch hole) work, references to which will be found later in this book.

Ireland

During the sixteenth and seventeenth centuries the Irish imported lace ruffs, collars and cravats from Flanders. Payment for these luxuries, however, was a severe drain on the economy, and in the early eighteenth century a few far-sighted Irishmen formed the Dublin Society to encourage bobbin lace manufacture in Ireland. For 30 years from 1743 the society offered prizes for home-produced Brussels Lace and Dresden Point; it also provided money for teaching bobbin lace making to workhouse children, and a great deal of Irish bobbin lace came from this source, though it was never made on an industrial scale.

The oldest lace-making industry in Ireland, which dates from 1820, was that of Carrickmacross. **Carrickmacross** lace is made by the appliquéing of fine muslin on to machine-made net. In the early 1840s too much of this lace was made, and it did not sell. The industry declined, but after the famine of 1846 it was revived to provide work.

Limerick is another lace based on machine-made net. This was also made in the early nineteenth century. (More about this lace can be found in Chapter 5 which deals with tambour work and net laces.)

The most beautiful and best known needlepoint lace of Ireland was **Youghal**

Point (Irish Point). This industry was also established as a result of the famine. The Mother Superior of the Presentation Convent in Youghal, County Cork, first taught herself to make needlepoint lace by unravelling a piece of Italian lace which she had acquired. She then taught the children in her convent school to make Youghal point, an art which has spread to many other parts of Ireland.

Crochet is the other important lace of Ireland. (For more information about Irish crochet see Chapter 15.) The crochet industry was established in 1845 in the Ursuline Convent at Blackrock, County Cork, from where it spread rapidly throughout Ireland. Irish crochet was used to make all types of collars and edgings. A beautiful dress made entirely of Irish crochet can be found in Cork Museum. (See figure 47.)

5 Popularity of Lace

Sixteenth century

In the first half of the sixteenth century lace was used very little by women and rather more by men, and lavishly by church dignitaries, both for personal adornment and for church linen.

Although Henry VIII wore very little lace, in his 1530 accounts there was an entry of five shillings and eight pence for a piece of 'yelowe lace'. He also had handkerchiefs and shaving cloths trimmed with 'Flandres worke', as well as 'coverpanes' and a handkerchief trimmed with 'Venice gold and silver'. Moreover, he bought his favourite wife, Jane Seymour, a 'perle edging' for her coif.

During the reign of his daughter, Mary I (1553–1558), some attempt was made to curb imports of cutwork into England by forbidding anyone who held rank lower than that of baron to wear ruffles made abroad. A lady who was unfortunate enough to be below the rank of a knight's wife was not allowed to wear any whitework or foreign cutwork.

It was during the reign of Elizabeth I (1558–1603) that lace became popular for decorating personal clothing. Elizabeth herself and her courtiers loved lace, and used it lavishly. The most spectacular adornments at the Elizabethan court were probably the neck ruffs, especially those of the Queen herself. They were bejewelled, spangled, bugled and pearled. They were made of cutwork, silver lace, gold lace, needlepoint lace and bone lace, and were made in single, double and treble layers.

Elizabeth is said to have been very fond of guipure lace for trimming ruffs and matching cuffs, but it is obvious from the many sixteenth century portraits that *Reticella* was also much in favour. Her courtiers liked lace with geometric designs.

They believed that fine clothes indicated a fine intellect. As Sir Phillip Sydney explained: the outside appearance was 'but a fair ambassador of a most fair mind'.

After starch was introduced into England from Flanders in 1564, ruffs became larger and larger. Elizabeth's coachman had a Dutch wife who had learnt the new art of starching, and it was she who first starched the Queen's ruffs. Before very long other refugees from Flanders set up starching establishments in England. Members of the court used them, but ordinary people avoided them, calling the starch 'devil's broth'.

In the damp English climate it was difficult to keep even heavily wired and starched ruffs in shape. Setting sticks, poking sticks and struts were used for fluting the ruffs. Iron poking sticks were used from around 1576 onwards; they were slipped into a holder and the folds of the ruff were formed over them as shown in

FIGURE 1
Sir Walter Raleigh by N. Hilliard, circa 1585. Reproduced by permission of The National Portrait Gallery, London

Diagram 2
Seventeenth century
goffering iron for
crimping lace ruffs
and frills

Commend me to your sister and tell her
that the lace I gave hir for Jackes ruff
was butt 15 yeards; if it be not enoughe,
as I think it is not, lett me knowe what
wanteth and I will send it, for there was
3 yeards left behind.

Anne and Mary Fytton, *Gossip in a
Muniment Room*, 1617

It is strange that so impracticable a
fashion lasted so long. Often women wore
a small extra lace frill sewn inside the large
ruff at the neck edge. At the French court,
Queen Margot had one ruff so large that
she had to send for a spoon over 60cm (2ft)
long in order to eat her soup at dinner.

As Elizabeth grew older and even more
vain, she wore higher and higher ruffs to
hide her yellowing neck, and no young
court beauty dared to risk the Queen's dis-
pleasure by wearing a ruff lower than that
of the sovereign. Elizabeth also prohibited
the common people from wearing ruffs
above a certain size. Trusty citizens were
stationed at all London's city gates with
strict instructions to cut down to size any
ruff which exceeded the permitted depth.
Few would risk having good lace ruined, so
most complied, keeping their large ruffs for
private gatherings outside the city. Again,
when she heard that apprentices had taken
to wearing white-work on their collars, the
Queen ordered the practice to cease
immediately; the first apprentice who disobeyed was to be publicly whipped in the
hall of his company.

Elizabeth did not confine her use of lace
to ruffs alone. She used it lavishly to
decorate clothing and household items
such as cushion cloths, tooth cloths, night
caps, doublets and veils. (A pair of lace
stocking fronts, similar to those worn by
Elizabeth, are in the Louvre Museum in
Paris.) The lace used by the Queen came
from Italy and Flanders as well as
England. From the Royal Wardrobe
Accounts we find that in the early part of
her reign she bought little lace herself, the
customary New Year gifts to the sovereign
accounting for much of the lace she wore.
One of her first gifts of lace came from Sir
Philip Sydney. Later he gave her a lace
smock. The Queen was said to have been
highly delighted with his original gift. She

diagram 2. In 1592 Elizabeth paid a black-
smith five shillings for a pair.

Enormous ruffs were also worn in the
French court of Louis XIV (1643–1715).
The French blamed the English for what
was a very uncomfortable fashion and
called it the 'English monster', while the
English, not to be outdone, blamed the
French and called it the 'French ruff'.
Often the ruffs were at least 23cm (9in.)
deep and measured more than 11m (12yd)
in length before they were fluted or
gathered.

With the introduction of starch,
materials for the ruffs became lighter;
cambric and lawn were used, often edged
with lace. Ruffs could be bought at haberdashers but were more frequently made at
home. A large household would hire a
seamstress, supply her with the necessary
materials, and she would make whatever
ruffs were needed. Considerable amounts
of lace, lawn and lace edgings were involved, as the following extract from a
letter written in the early seventeenth century indicates:

must have received many other gifts of lace over the years for it is not until the 1580s that Elizabeth's Royal Wardrobe Accounts show that she bought lace for herself: 'six yards of good lawn for ruffs, of cutwork and edged with white lace'. This cost her 60s (£3). After this, vast quantities of lace were bought in great variety. Unfortunately, all Elizabeth's accounts were made out in Latin which makes them very difficult to translate precisely, but we find crown lace, cheyne (chain) lace, byas lace, hollow lace, billament lace, diamond lace and Spanish chain, as well as bone lace and parchment lace (probably guipure). Elizabeth also used hair lace (*point tresse*).

Lace aprons and lace handkerchiefs also appeared in Elizabeth's reign. They appear to have been purely decorative. As one old rhyme put it:

> *Those aprons white of finest thread*
> *So choicelie tied, so dearly bought,*
> *So finely fringed, so nicely spread,*
> *So quaintly cut, so richly wrought.*
> Pleasant Quippes for Upstart
> Gentlewomen, 1596

One Elizabethan writer commented on the size and uses of the delicate lace-edged handkerchiefs:

> Maydes and gentlewomen gave to their favourites as tokens of their love, little handkerchiefs of about three or four inches square wrought about.
> *John Stow, 1526–1605*

These very small handkerchiefs, edged with gold lace, cost about 16d. (6½p) each. Cheaper ones, probably with thread lace, cost only 6d. (2½p) or 12d. (5p). When a gentleman was given such a favour, he wore it in his hat.

Although poorer people could not afford fine bone or point laces, or, indeed, would not even have been allowed to wear them, they did make cheap coarse laces for their own use. The French peasants of the sixteenth century made a narrow bobbin lace known as **Bisette**, and in the eighteenth century they produced **Gueuse**, which was known locally as 'beggar's lace'.

The common people of England wore **tawdry**, so called because it was tradi-

FIGURE 2
'A Flemish Lady' by Cornelius de Vos. Note the needlepoint handkerchief, deep lace cuffs and huge ruff made of lawn. Reproduced by permission of the Trustees, Wallace Collection, London

tionally sold at fairs held on St Audrey's (St Ethelreda) Day, 17 October. Ely, in Cambridgeshire, was granted a charter by Henry II to hold a fair on the anniversary of the saint's death and on the three following days. The tawdry lace sold at Ely fair was supposed to have touched the saint's shrine, and was eagerly bought by visiting pilgrims.

Until the early nineteenth century lace fairings sold at Ely fair were referred to as 'St Audrey's chains'. There are two traditional stories associated with the chains. One is that the saint pleaded so effectively for the life of a penitent thief that his chains were struck off, and he was freed. After this he became a monk and the chains were hung in Ely Cathedral. According to the second story, the saint, as a result of wearing necklaces or chains when she was young, developed a tumour on her neck. It is not known for sure precisely what tawdry lace was; it may have been a braid or ribbon, but tawdry is a word now accepted in the English language as meaning 'showy, and of little value'.

Elizabeth's cousin and greatest rival, Mary Queen of Scots, also wore a great deal of lace. She is said to have designed and made much of it herself during her tedious years of captivity. She was, without doubt, a very accomplished needlewoman, and much of her work is preserved in Oxburgh Hall in Norfolk. On the day of her execution in 1587 she went bravely to the block wearing on her head a 'dressing of lawn edged with bone lace' and 'a veil of lawn fastened to her cowl bowed out with wire and edged round about with bone lace'. On her effigy in Westminster Abbey she wears a lace-trimmed ruff.

Early seventeenth century

By the time of Elizabeth's death in 1603 interest in the arts was establishing itself in England, and in most great houses there was a 'frippery' or room set apart for family treasures. Lace often featured among the latter, for it was not only highly prized for its beauty but it was also extremely valuable. By the mid-seventeenth century special caskets were made in which to keep special pieces of lace. The caskets themselves were often covered with panels of needlepoint lace or embroidery.

Lace retained its popularity throughout the seventeenth century, and continued to be worn by both women and men. England's new monarch, James I, however, did little to foster this fashion, or any other innovation in dress for that matter. In 1604 Sir Anthony Weldon, Clerk to the Kitchen, summed up the new King's in-

Diagram 4
Top: shoe roses, early seventeenth century; bottom: lady's shoe with lace flounce, mid-seventeenth century

flexible nature and parsimonious habits as follows:

> In his diet and apparel and journeys he was very constant; as by his good will he would never change his clothes until worn to very rags; his fashion, never.

So impoverished was James's Scottish court that funds could not be found to provide his wife, Anne of Denmark, with a new and fashionable wardrobe suitable for her position as Queen of England. A selection from Elizabeth I's 3,000-gown wardrobe was sent to Scotland to be re-styled for the new Queen, who was highly indignant that gowns previously worn by a woman of 74 should be considered suitable for a blossoming young lady of 26. On her arrival in England the new Queen augmented her wardrobe by buying a large quantity of linen and lace, which included £5-worth of fine lawn ruff, and 16 metres (18 yards) of lace to trim it with. She also bought cutwork, 'great bone lace' and 'little bone lace' from Basing near Winchester, the 'great' and 'little' meaning wide and narrow respectively. The King, surprisingly, also purchased some 23 metres (25 yards) of lace for edging a ruff.

James was not only niggardly in matters

Diagram 3
Standing band circa 1600–1620

of his own personal adornment, he also forbade his servant girls to wear 'tiffany, velvet, lawns of white, wires on the head, or about the kerchief, koyfe, crest cloth, but only linen; no farthingale, the ruff restricted to four yards in length before the gathering or setting of it.' Apprentices fared no better, for James decreed that their gloves should not cost more than 1s. (5p) per pair and they should not be trimmed with gold, silver or silk lace, or ribbons. The royal restrictions on extravagant dress did not apparently extend to the sovereign's children: James's eldest son, the 14-year-old Henry, Prince of Wales, had no less than 31 pairs of richly-decorated and laced gloves.

Moreover, despite James's dislike of finery, shoe 'roses' and other ornaments blossomed in his reign. Shoe laces, also called cabbage shoe strings, were a development of the elaborate shoe ties worn in the early part of the seventeenth century. They were made of lace or ribbon, fashioned into rosettes, sometimes of considerable size. They were, moreover, extremely expensive. According to one 1619 source, they could cost 'from thirty shillings to three, foure and five pounds the pair'.* They failed, however, to impress the King. Sir Anthony Weldon records that when James I was confronted by footwear decorated with the fashionable roses 'he asked if they would make him into a ruff-footed dove; one yard of sixpenny ribbon served him that turn.' Ladies' shoes, although hidden by long skirts, were also decorated with lace roses similar to those of the men.

Men's garters of this period were quite different from the twentieth century's utilitarian pieces of elastic, as diagram 5 (right) indicates; they consisted of small sashes tied below the knee on the outer side in huge bows, sometimes decorated with lace or ribbon roses. They were made of expensive materials such as silk, cloth of gold or cloth of silver, and usually trimmed with deep lace ends. In 1616 Ben Jonson, in *The Devil is an Ass*, described this 'fine gartering' as being of 'scarlet, gold lace and cutwork.'

* Henry Peacham, *Truth of our Times*, 1638

Diagram 5
Left: falling band (collar), seventeenth century; right: wide sash garters with lace ends, seventeenth century

Boots, which up to the first decade of the seventeenth century had only been used for riding, were now fashionable for walking as well. They lent themselves to the extravagant use of lace. The lace was used either to decorate the turned down boot tops themselves, or it was attached to the tops of the boot-hose and allowed to fall over the boot tops. Boot-hose were worn to save the very fine silk stockings of the fashionable seventeenth-century gentleman from being chafed by the leather boot, and were made of linen or thicker silk.

Boots with cup-tops or bucket-tops which came into fashion about 1620 were particularly accommodating for lace. The very wide boot tops were filled with lace frills attached to the boot-hose tops. Sometimes linen frills edged with lace were used as alternatives to frills made entirely of lace. Boot-hose were always worn without garters to allow the lace frills to fall into the boot tops. About 30 years later boot tops increased to even larger proportions and allowed even more room for lace.

Although boot-hose and boot-hose tops were joined together they were usually charged for separately in accounts, because the lace trimming was so costly. In James Master's expense book of 1646–47 the following item appears: '. . . two yds of

Diagram 6
Boot with lace trimming, early seventeenth century

Diagram 7
Cup top boots with
lace boot-hose tops
circa 1620

Lace for Boothose Tops 11/-.' Just five years later he recorded: 'for 2 yards of lace for ye boothose tops £1.3.0.', which was over double the price paid for his first purchase.

So much lace on boot-hose tops caused unexpected problems: '. . . your tops . . . made such a rushing noise as you walk'd that my mistress could not hear one word of the love I made her . . .', wrote James Howard in *The English Monsieur*, in 1674.

Lace was also used for household purposes as well as for personal adornment. Seaming lace, sometimes called 'spacing lace', was used a great deal to join together narrow widths of linen to make sheets, cupboard cloths, pillow beres (cases) and so on. It was a strong narrow insertion lace which served instead of seams.

During James I's reign point laces and cutworks from Flanders and Italy were the height of fashion, and the King caused great distress in his own country by granting monopolies for the importation of foreign laces. English lace makers had reached the point of starvation when, on 8 April 1623, a petition was sent to the High Sheriff of Buckinghamshire from the people of Great Marlow in that county because of the 'bone lace-making being much decayed'.

James's queen, however, bought quantities of English lace. Apart from her earlier purchases at Basing, she paid £600 for a layette for her daughter Mary, which included 'six veils of lawn edged with bone lace; six gathered bibs of fine lawn with ruffles edged with bone lace;' and over £600 for laced linen for the 'lying-down' for the birth of her daughter Sophia. Unfortunately, little Sophia lived only three days but she has a stone monument in Westminster Abbey consisting of a stone cradle covered with lace trimmed sheets. Her little sister, Mary, who was scarcely two, died a year later and her effigy, with lace trimmed ruff, cap and cuffs, is close by.

James himself bought foreign laces: he paid over £16 for nine metres (ten yards) of needlepoint lace for edging his night caps and £5 for four cutwork night caps for his son, Prince Charles.

Throughout the first part of the seventeenth century the extravagant use of lace continued. At court the great neck ruffs were replaced by large, softly falling collars, which made life a lot easier. The virtues of the falling band (collar) were summed up as follows: '. . . you should chance to take a nap in the afternoon, your falling band required no poking stick to recover it.' (From John Marston's *The Malcontent*.) Once laundered, these bands were returned in special boxes, hence our present day expression 'band box fresh'. The falling collars were, moreover, ideal for displaying the lovely Venetian needlepoint laces to perfection. (See diagram 5, left.)

In 1625, when Charles I came to the throne, £1,000 was required for his lace and linen. By 1633, the bill had risen to

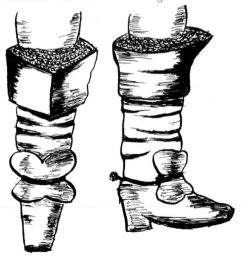

Diagram 8
Bucket top boots with
lace edged boot-hose
tops circa 1620

Diagram 9
Falling ruff circa 1625

Diagram 10
Double lace cuffs, late
sixteenth century or
seventeenth century

Diagram 11
Large lace collar or
whisk worn mid-
seventeenth century

FIGURE 3
Henrietta Maria by
H. Van Steenwyck.
Wife of Charles I.
Reproduced by
permission of the
National Portrait
Gallery, London

£1,500, whereupon it was resolved that this expenditure must be reduced to £1,000 again. Ironically the bills for lace, which were so nonchalantly run up, were seldom paid in full, for there were never sufficient funds in the royal coffers to meet them. In one very lean year, the royal lace merchants received precisely nothing.

Lace was used as the all-purpose decoration. There was no item of personal clothing or household linen that was too insignificant to be trimmed with it. Shirts, sheets, cuffs, collars, cushions, boot-hose tops and tooth cloths were all embellished. The 909 metres (994 yards) of lace bought for trimming 12 collars and 24 pairs of cuffs, and the 548 metres (600 yards) of 'fine bone lace' for the ruffs of the king's night shirts, are just two examples of this lavish use of lace.

Ladies' gowns were adorned with large lace collars, or whisks, sometimes wired at the back. Like their menfolk, they usually wore lace cuffs to match the collars, which they called 'handfalls'. Sometimes the cuffs were double. Gentlemen often wore a little muff on each wrist to protect their magnificent lace handfalls whilst playing cards.

Charles's French queen, the dainty Henrietta Maria, was a fashion leader among the ladies, who even trimmed their footwear with lace flounces. Their shoes, often green, or edged with green, were supposed to have wrought havoc in male hearts, even causing *The Tatler* to comment at length on the perils of looking at green lace, even the sight of which in the shoe-maker's window was said to create 'irregular thoughts and desires in the youth of this nation'. *The Tatler* further added that blue slippers with green heels were 'equally inflammatory'.

By the 1630s, lace was not only plentiful but very beautiful. It was generally wider and more heavily patterned than the earlier laces. English bobbin lace was near its peak of perfection and it was now the French who were seeking to buy lace from England. In 1636 the Countess of Leicester, whose husband was on a diplomatic mission in France, was asked by him to purchase English lace as a present for the Queen of France. The Countess promised to do her best, but tactfully pointed out that it was impossible for her to buy good English lace for the amount her husband was prepared to send, for she said 'these bone laces, if they be good, are dear, and I will send the best for the honour of my nation and my own credit'. She later wrote to say that she had bought the lace at a cost of £120, and that she must send it over quickly before it was out of fashion, because 'such things are being sent over almost every week'.

So good was English lace at this time that Henrietta Maria also sent quantities of it to her sister-in-law, Anne of Austria. But in spite of the excellence of English lace, large quantities of foreign laces were still being imported into England, principally from Venice, Valenciennes and Brussels. Charles I became worried when the home industry began to fail, and he made an effort to curb the imports of foreign lace by prohibiting the import of 'purles, cut-works, and bone laces'. This measure helped the home industry but encouraged smuggling.

Late seventeenth century

After the execution of Charles I in 1649 life in Cromwell's Commonwealth was a much more sober affair. The wearing of lace was discouraged, and lace collars, cuffs, handkerchiefs and boot-hose largely disappeared. Lace did not, however, vanish from the scene altogether, for the Royalists and the well born continued to use lace; the men wore lace edged cuffs and collars, while the ladies clung to their extravagant lace whisks or gorgets.

The Puritans adhered to the principal of 'plainness in all things'. But the Parliamentarians were not all Puritans, and even General Harrison, a prominent Cromwellian, appeared in public wearing silver lace and ribbons. Cromwell's daughter had her portrait painted decked out in the latest French fashion, while his mother was proud of her beautiful point lace handkerchief. On his death, Cromwell's body was splendidly arrayed in rich Flander's lace, velvet and ermine.

The Puritan ladies managed to satisfy their consciences and their love of lace by wearing lace representing religious subjects. The satirists quipped that 'they were religious petticoats and holy embroideries'. Lace-edged caps, or coifs, were worn under tall sugar-loaf Puritan hats.

The Commonwealth lasted for 11 sombre years until 1660, after which the English people enthusiastically welcomed back Charles II, 'The Merry Monarch', and an era of colour and luxury was introduced. All the carefully-hoarded lace was brought out and clothing refurbished. A

FIGURE 4
Margaret Conyers
circa 1640.
Reproduced by
permission of Norfolk
Museums Service,
Norwich

LA GALERIE DV PALAIS

Tout ce que l'Art humain a jamais inuenté
Pour mieux charmer les sens par la galanterie,
Et tout ce qu'ont dupas la Grace et la beauté,
Se desçouure a nos yeux dans cette Gallerie .
Bosse in n fe .

Jcy les Cavaliers les plus aduantureux
En lizant les Romans s'animent a combatre ;
Et de leur passion les Amans s'angoureux
Fla~nt les mouuemens par des vers dł'theatre

Jcy faisant semblant d'acheter deuant tous
Des gands, des éuantails, du ruban, des danteles;
Les adroits Courtisans se donnent rendez-vous,
Et pour se faire aimer, galantisent les Belles .

Jcy quelque Lingere a faute de juceez
A vendré abondamment de colere se picque
Contre des Chiccancurs qui parlant de procez
Empeschent les Chalands d'aborder sa Boutique
le Blond le jeune excud Auec Priuilege du Roy

gentleman was not considered well dressed unless he wore lace on his collar, cuffs, boot-hose, handkerchief and silk shirt. The women wore lace aprons, gloves, lace trimmed chemises, lace whisks, lace-edged neckerchiefs, and lace flounces on their shoes. They carried folding lace fans and lace edged handkerchiefs. The handkerchiefs were far too precious to use, and a weeping lady would allow her tears to drip inelegantly off the end of her nose rather than soil her lace handkerchief. Great was the distress if one were lost. Contemporary newspapers were full of advertisements appealing for the return of lace lost, but seldom found. The *London Gazette* in 1672 carried the following advertisement: 'Lost, a lawn pocket handerchief with a broad hem, laced round with a fine point

Diagram 12
Lace edged coif worn under sugar loaf hat circa 1645

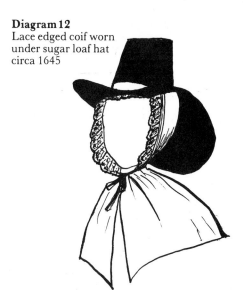

FIGURE 5
Cavaliers and their Ladies buying fans and books at a Paris bookstall. Engraving by A. Bosse. Photograph by permission of Radio Times Hulton Picture Library, London

lace about four fingers broad, marked with an R in red silk.' Another in the same publication in 1675 read: 'A right point lace with a long muslin neck laced at the ends with a narrow point about three fingers broad, and a pair of point cuffs of the same, worn foul and never washt, was lost on Monday last.' Very occasionally, honesty did triumph: 'Found in a ditch, four laced forehead cloths, one laced pinner, one lace quoif, one pair of laced ruffles.'

The large spreading collars, which showed off the Venetian points so well, went out of fashion when the flowing curly wigs were introduced. Falling down over the shoulders, the wig hid most of the collar. As a result, cravats became fashionable, and were worn until about 1735. They were made either entirely of lace, or linen edged with deep lace. Venice point continued to be used for trimming them. Charles II paid £194 to his lace merchant for three Venice point cravats.

The seventeenth century diarists, Samuel Pepys and John Evelyn, are very informative on the fashions of the period. Lace was indispensable to the small and dapper Samuel Pepys. On 8 October 1662 he records in his diary his delight with his new lace 'scallop' (a collar with scalloped edges), even though it cost him £3. He was so delighted in fact that he immediately ordered another, and on 19 October he

wrote: 'Lord's Day. . . . Put on my new lace band, and so neat it is that I am resolved my great expense shall be lace bands, and it will set off anything else the more.' But what was sauce for the gander was not sauce for the goose, for Pepys also recorded: 'My wife and I fell out about my not being willing to have her gown laced . . . at this she flounced away in a manner I never saw her, nor which I could ever endure.' Mrs Pepys had threatened that 'she would go and buy a new one and lace it and make me pay for it.' But lace also patched up some of Samuel's quarrels too, for, having fallen out with his wife, Elizabeth, over one of his amorous escapades, he salved his conscience by giving her money to buy lace.

Pepys also had an eye for fine lace decorating the clothing of other women. One day he saw the petticoats of the King's mistress blowing in the wind on a line, and wrote:

My wife and I to my Lord's lodging; where she and I staid walking in White Hall Gardens. And in the Privy Garden saw the finest smocks and linnen petticoats of my Lady Castlemaine's laced with rich lace at the bottom, that ever I saw, and it did me good to look at them.

John Evelyn, Pepys's contemporary, drew this delightful pen picture of ladies' fashions:

Short under petticoats, pure fine
Some of Japan stuff, some of chine
With knee-high Galoon bottomed,
Another quilted white and read;
With a broad Flander's lace below
Four pairs of bas de soye shot through
With silver; diamond buckles too,
For garters, and as rich for shoe,
Twice twelve day smocks of Holland fine,
With cambric sleeves rich point to join
(For she despises Colbertine).
Twelve more for night gown must adorn
With two point waitcoats for the morn
Of pocket mouchoirs, nose to drain
A dozen lac'd, a dozen plain;
Three night gowns of rich Indian stuff,
Four cushion-cloths are scarce enough
Of point and Flanders.

Mundus Muliebris, 169(

Diagram 13
Cornet or shadow made of lawn and lace, and lace edged neckerchief, seventeenth century

At the beginning of Charles II's reign, a great deal of lace was imported from Venice, France and Flanders for use in England. Brussels changed its designs to meet new fashions, and the lace was superb. It was at this time that English Point (*Point d'Angleterre*) was introduced. Charles tried to boost the home lace industry by reinforcing his father's ban on imports of foreign lace. The making of English point was a way round the ban, and met the court's insatiable demand for foreign lace. In 1662 Charles passed another Act banning foreign lace imports, which commented that the poor children of England were so good at lace making that foreign imports should be unnecessary. In spite of this, Charles himself granted a special licence for lace to be imported for 'the wear of the Queen, our dear mother the Queen, our dear brother James, Duke of York, and the rest of the royal family.'

One of Charles's last expenditures on lace was £20 for a cravat to be worn for the birthday of his 'dear brother'. One year later in 1685 this same dear brother became James II. In his short reign of three years he made little impression on lace fashions. James II wore a cravat of Venice lace for his coronation, and when he died in 1701 in exile in France he wore a laced nightcap. After that all good Jacobites aimed to die wearing a nightcap trimmed with lace.

James II's daughter, Mary, and her Dutch husband, William, were probably the most prolific royal spenders on lace. In 1694 Mary's bill for lace came to almost £2,000. Included in this bill were: '16 yards of lace for 2 toylights (toilets), £192; 24 yards of lace for 6 handkerchiefs, £108; 30 yards of lace for 6 night shifts, £93.' Another item was for about 13 yards of lace for 'combing cloths' costing £179, and '5¾ yards of fine broad cattgutt at 20s.', 'cattgutt' was probably a hair lace; it certainly was not cat gut. Mary also bought a wide variety of lace to make sleeve ruffles. Early in the reign, ladies' dresses had short wide sleeves showing the chemise sleeves which ended in deep lace ruffles, often of two or three layers. Aprons of richly coloured materials with lace frills

Diagram 14
Loosely tied lace edged cravat, second half seventeenth century

Diagram 15
Lace *fontange* and *steinkirk*, late seventeenth and early eighteenth century

were also worn.

During the 1690s the *fontange* or *commode* became fashionable. It was a high head-dress built up on a wire support and made of frill upon frill of lace and ribbon. The frills were attached to a close-fitting linen cap and the whole effect was rather similar to that of a half-closed fan. Lace streamers attached to the back or sides provided the finishing touches. The fashion originated in France with Mademoiselle Fontange, Louis XIV's mistress. When her curls escaped from the ribbon that held them while she was hunting one day, she hastily tied them up in a lace kerchief. Louis was so delighted by this impromptu coiffure that he begged her to wear it at court in the evening. She did so, and the *fontange* was born.

At first an attractive fashion, the *fontange* grew so high that it became uncomfortable and absurd, the butt of every contemporary satirist. The men complained that they looked like grasshoppers beside the women. Evelyn described these head-dresses in *Mundus Muliebris* in 1690 as follows:

> For tour on tour, and tire and tire,
> Little Steeple Bow, or Grantham Spire.

Although head-dresses, or 'heads' as they were usually called, were very expensive, costing between £30 and £50 each, one or two would probably last a woman her lifetime.

When buying lace, King William was no less extravagant than his wife. In 1690 his personal lace bill came to £1,603, and it increased every year until, in only six years, it had risen to over £2,500. On one occasion he bought 107 metres (117 yards) of cutwork for one dozen handkerchiefs. This cost him £485 – over £40 per handkerchief. Other expenditure on lace included £250 for six razor cloths, £158 for six point cravats, and £773 for 71 metres (78 yards) of lace to trim a further 24 cravats.

Cravats were then worn long and loose, and no gentleman was well dressed without one. English and French soldiers wore elaborate lace cravats as part of their uniform, and would not go into battle without their cravats or their silk stockings. One unkind wit suggested that the troops only wore their cravats into battle because they would not be seen dead without them, which was probably true. As one seventeenth-century writer put it:

> To war the troops advance
> Adorned and trim like females for the dance.

Steinkirks then became the rage; these were extra long cravats, the ends of which were pulled through a buttonhole or fastened with a long oval brooch. These brooches can still be found in antique shops. The fashion is said to have arisen after the battle of Steinkirk in 1692 when the French officers had no time to tie their cravats before going into battle, so hurriedly pulled them through a buttonhole instead. Steinkirks were always heavily laced, and were worn by all classes of people. Blandford Point and English lace made in Dorset was particularly popular for cravats, but at £30 a yard it was extremely expensive.

As well as their lace cravats, men wore full shirt sleeves ending in lace ruffles at the wrist, and their hats and summer gloves were all lace trimmed. Venetian ambassadors, visiting England in 1696, were warned that the only gifts really acceptable to the English were Venetian lace collars.

William's patronage helped the English lace industry to prosper, and in 1698 another Act was passed to prevent the importation of foreign 'bone lace, loom lace, needlework point and cutwork.' The penalty for infringing the law was the forfeiture of the lace concerned and a fine of 20s (£1) a yard. The Spanish rulers of Flanders immediately retaliated by prohibiting imports of English woollen goods into Flanders. This caused great distress in England, which was then a very large wool-producing and manufacturing country. England lost several hundred thousand pounds in revenue in exports of woollen goods. Caught between the distress of the English lacemakers who wanted to sell their product without foreign competition, and the wool producers who wanted to sell abroad, the English Parliament was forced to repeal the Act as far as Flanders was concerned.

When Queen Mary died, a victim of smallpox, in Kensington Palace in 1694, William resolved to put aside his lace-trimmed razor cloths and handkerchiefs for two years whilst in mourning. At the end of the two years he bought new lace, including £500-worth for trimming 24 new night shirts. William outlived Mary by eight years, and they lie together in Westminster Abbey, their effigies resplendent in lace. William's has a lace cravat and ruffles, and Mary's a raised Venice point tucker and double sleeves.

The reign of Queen Anne

When Anne came to the throne in 1702 Flanders lace was freely allowed into England, and the new Queen Anne used a great deal of it at her coronation. Lace was now becoming known by its place of manufacture, and for the first time the terms 'Brussels' and 'Macklin' appear in the Royal Wardrobe Accounts. English lace was also of good quality and the standard was boosted by the refugees from

France fleeing from religious persecution.

In the early eighteenth century huge amounts of gold and silver lace were used. Ladies even decorated their bright cherry-coloured stays with gold and silver lace. Points of Spain (*Point d'Espagne*) was used for all state garments, except for heads and ruffles, which required thread lace. Eventually the wearing of metal laces increased to such an extent that Queen Anne prohibited their import on pain of £100 fine and the forfeiture of the goods.

During Anne's reign English society ladies took to copying their French counterparts by receiving their visitors while still in bed in the morning. They were thus able to show off their lavishly laced-trimmed night wear, beds and bed linen. Lace continued to be immensely popular among all classes of people; some churchmen protested mildly when trades-men and valets began to deck themselves in lace, but their complaints were ignored. Even Quakers, who believed plainness a virtue, could not resist wearing lace, and earned themselves the name of 'wet Quakers'.

Queen Anne's favourite lace was Mechlin, which then cost about 13 shillings (65p) a yard. Men had by now become so used to spending large amounts in order to supply their womenfolk with lace that when a new vogue for things Chinese arrived many a husband thought the money he was supplying was for a new lace head, when instead he was paying for a new Chinese vase or punch bowl. A certain Thomas Clayton made this un-flattering entry in his accounts: 'Lace and fal-lalls, and a large looking-glass to see her old ugly face in – frivolous expenses to please my proud lady.'

The Georgian Period

Queen Anne died in 1714, and England entered the Georgian age, which lasted for 116 years and covered the reigns of four Georges, ending with the death of George IV in 1830. The second half of the Georgian era was a turbulent period in European history. During this time the Industrial Revolution took place in England; the Seven Years War with France

FIGURE 6
Mary Pettus by an unknown artist, circa 1730–40. She is wearing laced double ruffles with modesty piece and tucker to match. Photograph by courtesy of Norfolk Museums Service, Norwich

began in 1756; the American War of Independence started in 1775; the French Revolution began in 1789; and the Napoleonic Wars continued until 1815. Some of these events had a direct bearing on the lace trade, and the end of the eighteenth century marked the decline of the hand-made lace industry.

At the beginning of the Georgian period, however, elbow length sleeve ruffles were fashionable for ladies, and they remained so throughout most of the eighteenth century. Sometimes the ruffles were attached to the chemise sleeves and showed below the sleeves of the dress, or they were sewn to the dress itself but could usually be detached for cleaning. In the middle of the century, and again in the 1770s, the ruffles were very deep, and consisted of double and treble layers of lace, both on the dress itself or on the chemise sleeves. The *Weekly*

Register of 1735 gave this description of sleeve ruffles: 'Treble escalloped laced ruffles, one fall tacked up before and two down but all three down behind.' The French name for these ruffles, which was also commonly used in Britain in the Victorian era, was *engageantes*. The lace on them was matched on the cap, tucker or other neckwear.

Although an attractive and feminine fashion it was a very difficult one to wear elegantly, and caused many a problem for the unwary diner when eating soups and sauces.

Wrist ruffles for men were also popular at the beginning of the Georgian era. They were called 'weeping' ruffles, because the lace from which they were made was so deep that it hid the hands completely. It also formed a perfect hiding place for card sharps to conceal cards. Men also wore lace, or lace-edged, cravats until about 1735. Mechlin lace was very popular for these. George I had a favourite 'Macklin' cravat. Lady Mary Montagu, looking hopefully at her lover for a sign of his feelings for her, wrote: 'With eager beat his Mechlin cravat moves. He loves, I whisper to myself, he loves!'

The light delicate and dainty laces, such as Honiton, Brussels, Mechlin, Lille and the Bedfordshire, Buckinghamshire and Northamptonshire laces, were all ruffle laces. Valenciennes was also used for ruffles, but it was very expensive owing to the intricacy of its design. It was, however, a very strong lace, and because it stood up to hard wear and washing, it was used for undergarments and night wear. The heavy needlepoint laces had gone out of fashion for normal wear.

Lace, or lace-edged aprons, in fashion since Elizabethan times, were still worn in the mid-eighteenth century. The following advice is given in *The Recipe for Modern Dress* published in 1753: 'Frizzle your elbows with ruffles sixteen; furl off your lawn apron with flounces in rows.'

Lace was now held in such high esteem that even the murderess Margaret Caroline Rudd thought she might alter the course of justice when she appeared on trial at the Old Baily elegantly clad in a dress with lace flounces, lace sleeve ruffles, and a lace stomacher. The jury was deeply impressed but, nonetheless, found Margaret guilty and she was duly hanged.

The predilection for lace often dictated a way of life and death. Society ladies incurred vast debts with their lace merchants who often went bankrupt because of the non-payment of their bills. At the card tables many a lady, short of ready cash, would stake her lace handkerchief or cap instead, sometimes losing both. Her partner, if he were the perfect gentleman, would then stake both against her lace tucker, and allow her to win them back again. The rising suicide rate was an even more disastrous result of the preoccupation with lace. *The Connoisseur*, published in 1754–6, listed various causes for suicide, and suggested that a yearly bill of suicides should be published giving the reasons for the untimely deaths. Three of the reasons listed were French claret, French lace and French cooks.

When George II succeeded his father in 1727, Brussels and Mechlin were still the first choice for lace head-dresses, and all the light laces were used for the triple-tiered ruffles and lappets (strips hanging from an indoor head-dress). Gold lace flounces were also very much in fashion. Princess Mary, George II's daughter, had 'four fine laced Brussels heads, two looped and grounded and two point, ruffles, lappets, six French caps and ruffles' for her trousseau. English lace was also popular. When Frederick, Prince of Wales, married in 1736, his bride had a nightdress of

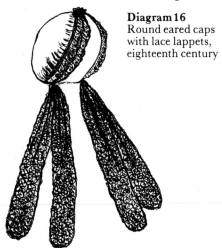

Diagram 16
Round eared caps with lace lappets, eighteenth century

exquisite English lace and he had a cap of the same lace. With the exception of one duke, the entire court wore English lace at the wedding.

From the 1730s women wore small frilled or lace coifs or caps on the top of their heads, which were often given the name of the lace from which they were made. There were 'trolly' caps, 'blonde' caps, 'Mechlenburgh' caps and 'Brussels' heads. Other lace-trimmed caps were known by their shape. A very popular one was the 'round-eared' cap. It was a very attractive little cap with a pinched-in brim and single or double lappets, often all of lace. Domestic servants wore single plain lappets tied under the chin. There were also little flat caps, known as pinners, with the lappets pinned on the top of the head. These were also frilled and lace trimmed.

George II did his best to encourage the home lace industry, and many a husband complained that his wife had squandered his money away on fine English lace, with the excuse that it 'set a great many poor people to work.'

George III, whose reign spanned the 60 years from 1760 to 1820, also tried to encourage the English lace industry. At the beginning of his reign he passed several Acts to curtail foreign imports, and as late as 1806 he levied a tax of £2 per yard on foreign lace. In spite of his efforts, in 1766 *The Dictionary of Commerce* accused English women of supporting Roman Catholicism by buying foreign lace:

> This but a few years since England
> expended upon foreign lace and linen
> not less than two million pounds yearly.
> As lace in particular is the manufacture
> of the nuns, our British ladies may as
> well endow monasteries as wear
> Flanders lace, for these Popish nuns are
> maintained by Protestant contributions.

By the end of the century, the English hand-made lace industry had suffered a further decline; machine-made net was already on the market, and in 1809 Heathcoat perfected his twist net machine which was to revolutionize the lace industry in Britain.

Women's clothes for most of the eighteenth century remained extravagant.

Hooped gowns and petticoats were lavishly trimmed with lace flounces, frills and ribbon bows, which the French called *échelles*. The gowns were generally cut with a low decolletage, filled in with a lace tucker or modesty piece. The tucker went right round the edge of the neckline, while the modesty piece was a strip of lace which went straight across the neck edge.

Until the French Revolution new English fashions usually originated in France and British women were kept in touch with the latest mode by fashion dolls. These dolls, often life-sized, called pandoras, moppets or poupees, were dressed in exact replicas of the latest fashions and

FIGURE 7
Wooden mannequin or fashion doll, circa 1815. Dress with tatted lace trimming. Photograph by courtesy of Norfolk Museums Service, Norwich

sent out by the leading French fashion houses in the days before fashion magazines.

With the elaborate gowns of the 1770s went equally elaborate hair styles. The hair was dressed very high over pads of horsehair and false curls and ringlets added, and the whole creation was topped by lace, ribbons, flowers, fruit or even more outlandish ornaments. The hair took many hours to dress and was kept in place by a paste of flour and tallow. Once done the edifice was not taken down for many weeks. In order to discourage mice and rats, ladies slept with their heads in metal frames. Long-handled head scratchers topped with small ivory hands were carefully inserted into the coiffures to relieve the itching caused by lice and other insects.

These unwieldy styles required larger lace caps to protect them, and so large mob caps, which women wore during the day to protect the hair, replaced the little lace coifs worn earlier in the century.

Silky, shimmering, blonde lace which had been introduced into Britain a few years earlier became popular in the 1770s for making mantles or cloaks.

In the late 1780s Anglomania hit France, and everything British was eagerly sought and bought. In 1788 English lace was considered an item of high fashion in Paris, and French women wore caps of English and French lace which were called 'The Union of France and England'.

After the French Revolution there was a radical change of ideas on both sides of the English Channel. In matters of dress, class distinctions became less obvious. Extravagant and showy clothes were despised, and the end of the century saw a dramatic change in both men's and women's fashions. The clothes of both sexes became much simpler.

More attention was paid to the cut of men's clothes and the quality of the material rather than to elaborate decoration and accessories. Vivid colours and lace trimmings disappeared. The lace-trimmed cravat was replaced by the stock, a plain strip of linen.

Women's clothes were designed on Grecian lines, and made of muslin and semi-transparent materials. Hoops and stays disappeared, and flesh-coloured under garments were worn to emphasise the natural figure. Tamboured sprigs and flowery trains decorated the high waisted muslin dresses, and their deep hems were embroidered with white-work. One of these fashionable dresses would have cost about 18s. (90p).

Demand for the heavy laces declined rapidly, for they were totally out of keeping with the new soft draperies. Only very light and blonde laces were used. Women turned from expensive hand-made lace to homespun trimmings and machine-made net. Many accessories such as gloves, mittens, collars, cuffs, fichus and bonnet trimmings were all home knitted in fine white cotton. During this period much of the old, heavy lace which was discarded was lost to posterity; a great deal was cut up to make other trimmings or for doll's clothes, and some was actually burnt. Fortunately, though, some of it was carefully hoarded.

The Victorian Era

The narrow flimsy dresses of the early nineteenth century gradually widened out at the hem, and the materials became more substantial until, in the 1860s, the other extreme was reached in the crinoline of the mid-Victorian era. Throughout the 1830s and 1840s Indian muslin continued to be used to make accessories and trimmings, and was decorated with tambour work and white work (as discussed in Chapter 15), which was also used to decorate the huge collars known as perelines, as well as cuffs, caps, collars, tippets and flounces.

Other laces made a comeback from 1830 and were also used for perelines and lace scarves, bonnet veils and wide dress flounces. Black Chantilly was fashionable for edgings. Nightwear and underwear were trimmed with Valenciennes. Also fashionable were lace fans, folding carriage parasols and large handkerchiefs, sometimes as much as 64cm (25in.) square.

In the 1860s there was a black and white phase, and black Chantilly was in demand, especially for the huge shawls which were large enough to drape down over the very wide crinolines.

Under their often unmanageable crinolines, for modesty's sake, Victorian women took to wearing pantaloons, or long white drawers, which reached down to the calf. They were lace trimmed, Valenciennes being popular because of its washability. Little girls wore pantalettes which reached down to their ankles, the lace frills on the legs peeping charmingly beneath their skirts. Quite often they wore false pantalettes, which consisted of two straight legs frilled at the ankles but reaching only above the knees, where they were held in place with elastic.

Machine-made Valenciennes came onto the market in 1840, and was a fairly good imitation of the real thing. Chantilly lace was also made by machine from 1840. Over the next 20 years so much machine-made lace became available that by 1860 it had become so cheap that a square yard of plain net cost only 6d. ($2\frac{1}{2}$p).

Until 1870 lace caps and lappets were worn by middle-aged and elderly women, and bonnet veils were also worn. Small lace Peter Pan collars decorated the crinoline bodices. The heavier crochet laces, particularly Irish imitation Venetian lace, as well as Duchess and Alençon laces were now widely used.

Queen Victoria was a great collector of lace, and when she died her lace collection was valued at £76,000. After The Great Exhibition of 1851, where some very fine examples of both hand-made and machine-made lace were on display, a committee of experts was formed to collect items for a more permanent exhibition, which became the Victoria and Albert Museum in London. The committee selected a number of items which were displayed at Marlborough House in May 1852. When Queen Victoria visited the exhibition she was thoroughly dismayed to find that only one piece of lace was on show, and she promptly offered to lend a number of pieces from her own collection.

By the end of the nineteenth century machine-made lace had virtually replaced the hand-made variety. There was little now that could not be satisfactorily imitated by machine. Hand-made lace

ceased to be produced on a commercial scale, although it still survived as a hobby. Crochet, cutwork and Venetian lace was all machine made. Ecru was now a popular shade, and much old lace was dyed with coffee to keep it fashionable. Hand-made laces that continued to be produced were usually Torchon or Bedfordshire-Maltese. These could be made relatively quickly, and still had a market in shops where the customers could afford the real thing.

The sewing machine had been invented by the end of Victoria's reign and it is interesting to notice how retailers clearly distinguished between garments made by hand with real lace and those made by machine with machine-made lace.

The following items and prices are typical of those advertised in Harrods' first catalogue published in 1895: hand-made cambric nightdresses lavishly trimmed with real Torchon lace sleeve frills, lace yokes and neck frills, cost from 12s. 6d. to 18s. 6d. ($62\frac{1}{2}$p to $92\frac{1}{2}$p); cambric chemises (which took the place of vests), trimmed with real Torchon cost 3s. (15p) if made by machine, and between 4s. and 11s. (20p and 55p) if sewn by hand. There were also camisoles at around 5s. (25p) and combinations at 9s. 6d. ($47\frac{1}{2}$p), all heavily trimmed at neck, sleeves, and legs with lace edging, insertion lace and ribbons.

Long waist slips known as skirts, made out of a type of calico called long cloth, were elaborately trimmed at the hem with deep lace frills and lace insertions. The prices of these ranged from 6s. to 22s. (30p to £1.10p) depending on whether the lace was real or imitation. There were knickers and drawers at about 6s. (30p) a pair; lace caps and head-dresses which cost 4s. (20p) each; lace capes from 7s. to 23s. (35p to £1.15p); lace jabots; veils and collar bands with lace fans and frills. There were black silk stockings with lace fronts from 8s. to 16s. (40p to 80p). There were also tea gowns with leg-o'-mutton sleeves, and deep lace shoulder frills.

Also featured in the catalogue were cutwork table cloths, called 'five o'clock' cloths. They cost from about 5s. (25p) depending on the amount of cutwork. The one shown in figure 8 would have

Diagram 17
Cambric chemise trimmed with 'real' Torchon lace, 1895

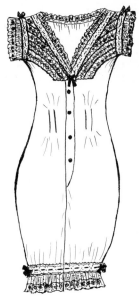

Diagram 18
Cambric combination trimmed with 'real' Torchon lace, 1890. These replaced the chemise in the late nineteenth century

been very expensive, and the owner has crocheted a lavish lace edging with a wheatear pattern.

Sunshades and parasols such as the one shown in figure 9, were also advertised. The following is an example: 'Sunshade, in black moire, lined cream or the new leather coloured lace 12/9–25/6.' Other fashionable colours for lace in the 1890s were butter, cream and ecru.

Lace was also advertised by the yard as the following examples show:

'Real Valenciennes edging $4\frac{3}{4}$d to $1/6\frac{1}{2}$d per yard. Insertion $7\frac{3}{4}$d to $1/6\frac{1}{2}$d per yard.'

'Real Honiton laces 2/3d to 12/9d per yard. Flouncing 36/- to 5 guineas per yard.'

'Duchess laces 3/11d to 40/- per yard. Flouncing 45/- to 5 guineas per yard.'

'Real lace handkerchiefs in Duchess, Honiton, Point Gaze, Valenciennes 4/11 to 25/- each.'

'Real Torchon lace suitable for trimming skirts and costumes $1\frac{3}{4}$d to $8\frac{3}{4}$d per yard.'

'Guipure lace 5 inches wide 4/11.'

In order to compare these prices with those of today, one yard is approximately 90cm, and one shilling (1s. or 1/-) is equal to 5p. Until well into the twentieth century any purchase of lace or haberdashery which came to an odd three farthings ($\frac{3}{4}$d.) meant that the customer would receive a packet of pins instead of a farthing ($\frac{1}{4}$d.) change.

Twentieth century

The Edwardian period which followed Victoria's death in 1901 was one of extravagance and ostentation, at least for those in high society, for they followed the example of King Edward VII.

The female silhouette was an S-shape, with a large bust and protruding bottom, achieved with the aid of a special straight-fronted corset. Skirts fell smoothly over the hips to a bell-shaped hem. Dresses and gowns were fussy creations of crêpe-de-Chine, tulle and chiffon lavishly trimmed with lace. Day gowns had high lace collars reaching right up to the ears and often falling down over the shoulders. The collars were boned to keep them standing. Long, tight sleeves finished at the wrists

Diagram 19
Tea gown 1895

FIGURE 8
Tablecloth with Teneriffe cutwork insertions and deep crochet edging. Late nineteenth century.

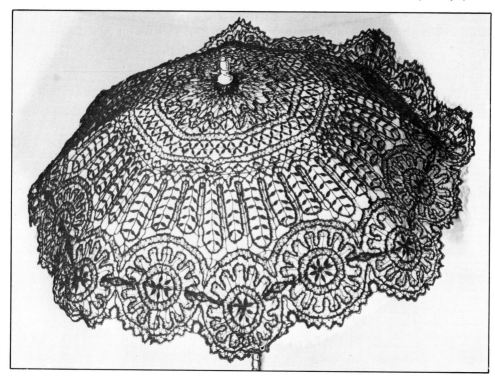

FIGURE 9
Black Bedfordshire-
Maltese lace parasol.
Nineteenth century

with lace cuffs or lace frills which reached half-way over the hands. Evening gowns were low cut, trimmed with wide lace at the neck and sleeves. The skirts of both day and evening gowns were trimmed with lace or braid. The tea gowns of the Victorian era were still worn and blossomed into artistic creations of lace and frills. Blouses were fussy with cascades of lace frills and tucks. Petticoats, underwear, night wear and baby wear were all lace trimmed.

Machine-made lace was, of course, now freely available and cheap, but for some reason it was not popular with the rich. They preferred to use the real hand-made lace but, unfortunately, it was not made in any quantity. Crochet lace was very much in vogue, especially the raised Irish type.

In contrast to the rather frivolous lace-trimmed gowns, tailor-made clothes were also fashionable, especially with the middle class girls who were beginning to work as typists, shop assistants and governesses where fussy clothes would have been impracticable.

At the end of Edward's reign in 1910 there was a fundamental change in fashion. Skirts became narrow, and bodices became softly draped. Lace went out of favour as a trimming and buttons were used instead, being sewn on almost anywhere.

From this time on lace was used less and less, especially during the First World War (1914–1918).

During the Second World War (1939–1945) clothing restrictions were in force and people were given clothing coupons, which were sufficient only for the basic needs. Clothing, in fact, carried a 'utility' stamp. It was of fairly good quality, but was plain, without trimming or decoration.

After the war new synthetic threads gradually came onto the market and were used to make nets and laces. They were far more durable than the old cotton and linen laces and, of course, were easy to launder. The cotton laces needed ironing and, if not done carefully, were often pulled out of shape.

Perhaps one of the most useful types of lace today, compared with the purely decorative types, is the stretch lace which is popularly used for foundation garments.

6 Lace for Special Occasions

Weddings

Weddings and lace seem to go together, but the traditional white wedding began as recently as the nineteenth century.

In the weddings of the sixteenth century 'bride-laces' are mentioned as being carried aloft by the bridesmen, and there is much speculation as to what they really were. The weddings of the sixteenth century were very rumbustious affairs, when the bride was traditionally stripped of her garters, ribbons and fripperies at the altar by the young men, who often threw her to the ground in the process. The bride, therefore, chose two or three coloured garters as 'trophies', and kept them hidden in her bosom to distribute to the young men hoping that she might then retain those on her legs. The coloured garters or bride-laces chosen by the bride were worn round the sleeves of the gallant young bridesmen, or carried aloft as banners on branches of rosemary or broom. These bride-laces were made of buckram.

In 1575 Elizabeth I attended a wedding when she visited Kenilworth. At this wedding the bridesmen carried 'two broad bride-laces of red and yellow buckram, begilded'. Each of the 'lusty lads and bold bachelors' had his blue bride-lace on green broom tied to his left arm for 'on that side lies the heart'.

In the seventeenth century when Charles II married his Portuguese princess, he was very elegantly clad in petticoat breeches with a frill of lace 30cm (1ft) deep flounced out from the knee. His bride, Catherine of Braganza, wore a richly-coloured dress with a low cut lace collar and puffed sleeves. The skirt of the dress had lighter lace-trimmed panels at each side and was worn over a large farthingale, which was thought by diarist Samuel Pepys to be monstrously old fashioned.

In 1768, Godwin, a waiting woman of Lady Cowper (cousin of the incomparable letter writer, Mrs Delaney) got married. Lady Cowper wrote to her cousin: 'Godwin wore a white spotted satin cloak, and bonnet trimmed with blond, new lace handkerchief and ruffles upon gauze and a clear apron.'

Another interesting eighteenth-century wedding was that of a certain Joseph Nollekens, a famous sculptor, who married a lady called Miss Welch in 1772. The miserly sculptor (he left £200,000 when he died) was married in lace that he had smuggled into Britain from Italy in a plaster cast two years earlier. A contemporary described him as wearing 'lace ruffles and frills, the whole of which articles he had brought from Rome. His hair was dressed with curls on either side . . . and finished with a small bag tied as closely as possible to his neck.' The bag contained his money, and from all accounts, his neck was none too clean.

Most eighteenth-century bridegrooms spent as much on their wedding finery as their brides did; £500 for a coat and lace-trimmed linen was not at all exceptional. Miss Welch's father spent the considerable sum of £200 on her trousseau and wedding outfit. She wore 'an elegant point lace apron, rather unfashionable at this date but worn in memory of her mother [and] a small point lace cap to match the apron and ruffles.'

A fascinating list of items for a trousseau appears in Robert Southey's *Commonplace Book*. He says it was given to him by Sir Edward Littleton who believed the list to have been written by his mother in the late eighteenth century. The following list appears under linen:

A Brussels laced head ruffles,
handkerchief and tucker

A sute of Brussels drest night cloaths,
and rufles

A Macklen-face lace drest nigh cloaths,
and hancerchieef

A Paries cap, double hankerchieff and
fuffles

A dormoizeen mobb and tucker edged

A pinner and quoiff of face lace,
Macklen double ruffles,
handkerchieff and a hood of muslem
edged

A plain cambrick head ruffles and
tippett and tucker

A cambrick apron, a spoted cambrick
apron

A plain cambrick apron, a lawn apron

In the early nineteenth century, lace wedding veils became fashionable. In the 1830s and 1840s they were rather small but made of the most expensive lace that the bride's family could afford. Honiton and Brussels lace was the most coveted but if these were too expensive, Valenciennes and Alençon were favoured as second best. Mechlin was also popular, but the poorest bride's family only bought her blonde lace.

In Charlotte Bronte's *Jane Eyre* Jane considers a plain square of 'unembroidered blond' good enough for her 'low born head'. Mr Rochester thinks otherwise and sends to London for a 'priceless veil'. A splendid surprise for Jane, which turns to horror when the lovely lace is torn in two by the frenzied Mrs Rochester who drapes it over her purple swollen face and gazes at her awful reflection with bloodshot eyes. Jane went to her wedding with the square of blond pinned to her hair with a brooch.

It was usual for costly lace wedding veils to be kept as family heirlooms and handed down through the family to be worn by successive brides. Queen Victoria wore her own lace veil and wedding lace many times after her wedding. The dress itself was of Spitalfields satin, and the lace for the dress and veil was woven in the village of Beer, near Honiton. Two hundred lace-makers worked on it and the cost was £1,000. Even so, public opinion of the monarchy was so low in the early 1840s that four days before

Victoria's wedding, *The Times* published the following letter from 'a dressmaker':

> The papers constantly announce that the dresses of Her Majesty's court are composed wholly of British Manufacture. . . . The assertation is wholly unfounded. Her Majesty's dressmakers and milliners are foreigners and no other find favour at her court.
> . . . I am told that five of Her Majesty's vans were loaded at the Customs House.
> . . . I believe it is also understood that Her Majesty's dress is to be Brussels Lace instead of Honiton Lace though Honiton Lace has been purchased as a blind.

During Victoria's life much of the lace was taken off her wedding gown and used for other purposes, but the gown is displayed in the Museum of London with the original lace sleeve flounces and bertha. Substitute lace replaces that taken off. Victoria was scarcely 1.52 metres (5 feet) tall so the dress is tiny, and has a full pleated skirt and a low cut bodice. Her lace veil was quite small, only 1.37 metres (1½ yards) square.

She wore the same veil at the age of 74 for the wedding in 1893 of her grandson, George, Duke of York, later George V. She wore it with a little coronet over 'light black stuff'. The bride, Princess May of Teck, later Queen Mary, also wore a lace-trimmed dress. Her veil of Honiton lace belonged to her mother who had worn it in 1866. It was very small and rather out of date. A lady-in-waiting to the Tecks was quite disgusted and wrote in her diary, 'her veil hung in a little tiny narrow strip but a couple of inches wide quite at the back of her head only like an elongated lappet.' This despised Honiton veil, however, was worn by a third royal bride in 1904, by Princess Alice, a granddaughter of Queen Victoria.

Victoria's eldest daughter, the Princess Royal, was married just after her seventeenth birthday, and she made a beautiful bride with a dress of 'white moire antique with three flounces of Honiton lace'. The train, made of the same material, was over 2.74m (3yd) long, also trimmed with two rows of Honiton lace. Queen Elizabeth,

the present Queen Mother, borrowed another family veil from Queen Mary when she married the future George VI in 1923. It was a much larger veil than the 'elongated lappet', and was made of old *point de Flandres*. Age had turned it to a soft shade of ivory, and the wedding dress was dyed to tone with it.

Princess Alexandra had a new wedding veil for her marriage to the Honorable Angus Ogilvy, but it was trimmed with a border of old Valenciennes lace which had belonged to her grandmother, Princess Nicholas of Greece. Most modern royal brides now have new veils in keeping with the designs of their dresses. The present Queen, Princess Margaret and Princess Anne all had crisp full wedding veils of machine-made tulle net.

Funerals

As in many other countries, it was the custom in Britain to be buried in one's best clothes or full official regalia. In earlier centuries the sumptuary laws applied even to the dead. A seventeenth-century Act decreed:

No corpse of any person (except those who shall die of the plague) shall be buried in any shirt, shift, sheet, or shroud . . . other than that what is made of sheep's wool only . . . or be put into any coffin lined or faced . . . with any material but sheep's wool only.

This Act was in force till late in the eighteenth century but little notice was taken of it. It was outwardly complied with by wrapping the corpse first in a linen shroud and then in a woollen outer cloak.

It was considered a great privilege and an honour to be buried in lace. Even highwaymen thought it their duty to give the crowd a good show by wearing their very best clothes to the gallows. If he was to be hanged it was the highwayman's ambition to be hanged in lace. One gentleman of the road even rode to the gallows dressed in his very best lace sitting on top of his own coffin to give the public a better view.

Mrs Oldfield, a famous eighteenth-century actress and a great collector of lace, refused to be buried in wool. When she died in 1730, Pope in his *Moral Essays* immortalised her story thus:

Odious! in woollen. 'Twould a saint provoke!
(Were the last words that poor Narcissa
*   spoke.)*
No, let a charming chintz and Brussels lace
Wrap my cold limbs, and shade my lifeless
*   face;*
One would not, sure, be frighful when one's
*   dead –*
And – Betty – give this cheek a little red.

She had her wish for she was buried in Westminster Abbey in a Holland shift with a tucker of double ruffles, and a fine Brussels lace head.

The custom of burying people in lace was also widespread in Mediterranean countries. In the Ionian islands of Greece a great deal of beautiful lace lay interred with the dead for many hundreds of years. In the nineteenth century the Greeks robbed the graves and sold the lace to British officers stationed on Corfu. The lace was black and stinking when taken off the corpses, but in this state it was judged to be genuine. When the supply of grave lace ran out, the robbers began to sell cheap, coarse lace dyed to look old and decayed. In Spain the grandees were buried in rich clothes and fine lace but the common people were usually buried in clothes belonging to some religious order. In Sweden, Denmark and other northern European countries, it was customary to bury the dead in their richest and most cherished clothes. Quite often a small fortune in lace was interred with the corpse. Many European women chose to be interred in their wedding lace, and Queen Victoria's wedding veil was laid over her face after her death.

Christenings

Christenings were also occasions which called for lace. There was one dreadful christening in the eighteenth century when the baby was smothered by a mountain of lace. George III and Queen Charlotte were sponsoring a child of the nobility; at the end of the ceremony the Archbishop of Canterbury handed the child to its nurse remarking that it was the most docile baby he had ever christened. No wonder! The baby had actually suffocated in her lace clothes. This terrible episode was discussed in *Cornhill Magazine* in 1864 in an article called *Gossip on Royal Christenings*.

7 Smuggling

If you wake at midnight and hear a horses's
    feet
Don't go drawing back the blind, or looking
    in the street,
Them that asks no questions isn't told a lie
Watch the wall, my darling, while the
    Gentlemen go by.

Five and twenty ponies
Trotting through the dark
Brandy for the Parson
'Baccy for the Clerk;
Laces for a lady, letters for a spy
And watch the wall my darling, while the
    Gentlemen go by!

If you do as you've been told, likely there's
    a chance
You'll be given a dainty doll all the way
    from France,
With a cap of Valenciennes, and a velvet
    hood –
A present from the Gentlemen along o'
    being good!

                    Rudyard Kipling

Smuggling was a perennial problem for nearly all lace producing countries. There are many fascinating stories connected with lace smuggling, especially in the early eighteenth century. Many thousands of pounds were made from smuggled lace, particularly by the wealthy upper classes.

Lace was often smuggled into England in coffins, with or without the corpse. The occupant of the coffin was supposed to have died whilst on the continent. The body would then be brought home for burial in England, the burial service performed, and the coffin duly interred. Later, the sorrowing 'relatives' would visit the grave, usually at night, to remove the smuggled lace from the coffin. Sometimes the lace was packed round the corpse. In 1732, when the Bishop of Atterbury was brought home for burial in Westminster Abbey, the High Sheriff of Westminster found, secreted in the coffin, £6,000-worth of French lace! Often there was only lace and no body at all. On one occasion the coffin of a dead clergyman was found to contain a head, hands and feet, the body having been replaced by lace. Most of the coffin tricks became well known to the customs officials and they not only opened any coffin brought into the country, but gave the corpse a thorough prodding.

From 1751 onwards customs officials made a determined effort to stamp out lace smuggling, and they raided homes, shops and offices. During one such raid in the winter of 1752 they searched a tailor's shop and found a large quantity of gold, silver and other laces. As a result the tailor was fined £100, and all his lace was burnt.

In 1764 George III made a personal stand against smuggling by ordering that no foreign lace was to be worn at the forthcoming marriage of his sister, Augusta. His order was largely ignored, and three days before the wedding a large amount of foreign lace was seized from the court milliner by ever vigilant customs officials. The milliner, who was French, hastily retired to France taking with her the £11,000 she had made from smuggling.

In the same year customs men made another haul of lace weighing over 45kg (100lb.). It was all burnt. After this members of the aristocracy were more cautious, and wore only English lace for public functions. There were many newspaper reports about seizures of smuggled lace and the ingenious hiding places found for it. A loaf of bread was found to contain £200-worth of lace. A Turk's turban revealed another £90-worth. Books, bottles, parasols and even babies were all used as aids for hiding lace. The customs men were known to stop carriages and relieve the occupants of all their lace garments; they even removed the lace gloves from ladies as they walked down the street. Six pairs of ruffles and 11 metres (12 yards) of lace edging were confiscated from a footman. A gentleman from the Spanish Embassy handed over 36 dozen laced trimmed shirts, numerous sets of ruffles, and dozens of other items of lace for ladies' wear.

One of the Customs men's biggest coups in the infamous year of 1764 involved 'a person of the highest quality' and consisted of 16 cloaks trimmed with lace; 10 pairs of ruffles, 6 pairs of ladies' blond ruffles and 25 pairs of gentlemen's ruffles, 11 black lace handkerchiefs; 6 lace hats; 6 lace aprons and 24 lace caps.

The following year a number of English lace makers joined the Spitalfields silk workers in a demonstration demanding the prohibition of foreign goods. They marched to Westminster with banners bearing long strips of lace or silk. On being told that nothing could be done until the next session of Parliament they expressed their anger by smashing up the Duke of Bedford's fences on their way home. On a later occasion, when the lace makers met the members of the House of Lords, they found that the latter wore lace only of English manufacture. No doubt the wily

Members of Parliament had been forewarned against wearing foreign lace, thus leaving the English lace makers with no grounds for complaint.

During the latter part of the eighteenth century and the early part of the nineteenth century a vast amount of lace was smuggled into France from Belgium, using large dogs as carriers. A dog would be acquired in France and treated as a well-loved pet. It would be well fed and well treated so that it was completely faithful to its owners. The French owner would then take the dog across the border into Belgium to a new owner. The Belgian owner would then tie the dog up and starve it until it was almost a bag of bones. When it was thoroughly emaciated, it was wrapped round with yards and yards of lace and a skin from a larger dog fitted over it. The dog was then released at the border to find its way back to its French owner. Dogs were able to carry up to 12kg (26lb.) of lace in one journey. Eventually the French Customs stopped the flow of contraband lace by offering a reward for every dog captured. Between 1820 and 1836 well over 40,000 dogs were destroyed.

In spite of all the measures taken to put an end to smuggling, it continued until the free-trading policies of the nineteenth century were established, and made it unnecessary.

8 Bobbin Lace as a Cottage Industry

In the second half of the seventeenth and most of the eighteenth centuries lace making was essentially a cottage industry and the bulk of the lace was made by women and children. The women's earnings supplemented the men's meagre agricultural wages but, as mentioned earlier, the men themselves often made lace after coming home from a day's work in the fields. There were also a number of men who were employed as full time lace makers. In the seventeenth century many clergymen and non-conformist teachers who had been forced to give up their livings in the church took up lace making as a livelihood. Sailors often made lace while on long voyages, and sometimes while on shore leave as well.

Once the lace had been made by the cottagers it had, of course, to find its way to customers who could afford to buy it. This is where the lace dealers or lace manufacturers, as they preferred to be called, were important. They were the middle men who provided the link between the workers and their customers. The dealers went to the London lace markets once a week and sold the lace to the city's milliners and haberdashers, returning home with stocks of thread and silk for the lace workers to make up according to orders. At that time the weekly London lace markets were held at the George Inn, Aldersgate Street, and The Bull in the Mouth, St Martins by Aldersgate. Lace markets were also held regularly in all the lace making counties, and the dealers would also visit these as well as many of the large annual fairs which had become well established throughout the country. At the fairs, each of which was famous for its own speciality, the lace dealers bargained for, and bought, thread which they supplied to the lace workers. They also took orders for lace. Although pedlars usually carried among their supplies of pins, needles, ribbons and braids a certain amount of coarse lace, the most beautiful lace was always made to order through the dealers.

Visitors to the lace making counties of Buckinghamshire, Bedfordshire and Devonshire, were often sold the laces of the area by waiters at the local inns where they stopped on their travels, or by serving girls who waited for travellers' carriages to arrive at the inns so that they could climb up to the carriage windows to offer their lace for inspection. Rarely did visitors continue on their way without having made a purchase.

Retail shopping as we know it did not exist before the seventeenth century. It developed as a result of greater demand for and more plentiful supply of goods, occasioned by a rapid growth in the population of London which increased by more than 300,000 between 1550 and 1650. The flamboyance and extravangance of the Elizabethan court set in motion an ever growing demand for luxury goods, particularly those connected with dress and personal adornment. In the sixteenth, seventeenth and early eighteenth centuries, fine fabrics, jewellery, leatherwork and lace were hand-made by skilled craftsmen and were, therefore, expensive. These items all came into the luxury goods class. London, centre of court and commercial life and home of some of the wealthiest people in the country, inevitably attracted luxury goods of both home and foreign manufacture, and as the seventeenth century progressed retail shops became established in the capital to sell these commodities.

As those selling similar wares tended to group themselves together, each row or

FIGURE 11
Eighteenth century
trade card.
Reproduced by the
permission of the
Trustees of the British
Museum, London

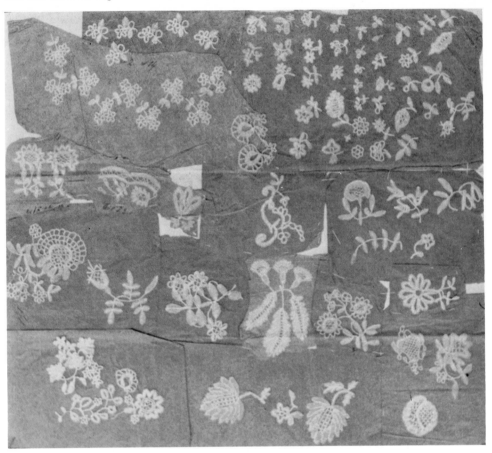

FIGURE 12
Sheet of Honiton
sprigs as collected by
the lacemen from the
workers. Nineteenth
century

street of shops becoming known for its particular merchandise. Cannon Street was famous for linen, Cordwainers' Street for hosiery, and Paternoster Street for lace and silk. It was to these establishments that the dealers took the lace they had collected for sale. They also took with them a sample book of patterns, similar to the one shown in figure 13, to obtain further orders.

When the bobbin lace industry was at the height of its prosperity, from the end of the seventeenth century until about 1770, the lace dealers provided work for over 100,000 lace makers. One Midlands dealer had 300 lace makers working for him at one time.

Unfortunately, the organization of the lace industry made the workers almost completely dependent upon the dealers, for the latter not only supplied the necessary thread but also the patterns. Lace workers, however, had a modicum of free-

dom, for they were not obliged to work exclusively for one dealer, provided that they did not use the patterns of one dealer to make lace for another.

Many lace dealers became very wealthy men, often by paying their workers a mere pittance, and by charging their wealthy customers an extremely high price for the finished lace. By the end of the seventeenth century a dealer's turnover could be as much as £50 a week, a considerable sum of money in those days. Documents in the Bedfordshire and Buckinghamshire Record Offices show that during the seventeenth, eighteenth and early nineteenth centuries some lace dealers left quite substantial amounts of money in their wills.

Many dealers were hard taskmasters, and were thoroughly hated by the workers, but the latter had almost without exception to rely solely on the local dealer for their supplies of thread. The thread often

FIGURE 13
Lace dealer's sample book, West Northamptshire, 1825–28. Point and wire-ground patterns. Reproduced by permission of Luton Museum and Art Gallery, Luton

cost them more than 10 per cent of their earnings on which the dealer was probably making a further profit. Often the local lace dealer also kept the only provisions shop in the village, and his lace workers were forced to accept the dealer's goods instead of money as payment for their work. These truck payments, as they were called, went on all over the country, and were not confined to the lace industry. Although illegal, they were still widespread in early Victorian times.

By the end of the eighteenth century the number of lace dealers had diminished considerably, which meant that those still in business dealt with many more workers. They often supplied all the lace-making materials, including threads and patterns, but they did not always buy back the finished lace. Independent lace collectors, some of them women, also set up in business, and they collected lace from the workers and resold it to the dealers.

In all the lace villages there was usually a 'cutting-off day' every four or five weeks. On this day the workers cut the lace off their pillows and took it to the dealer or his agent who would meet them at some such place as the village inn. In some villages, where the dealer was also the local shopkeeper, the workers took the lace direct to the shop. This could be an unpleasant experience for a lace maker whose work was not up to standard. In one Bedfordshire village the dealer kept a drawer slightly open, and if the work was badly done he would deliberately pinch the lace maker's fingers in it. On the other hand particularly good work earned the gift of a bobbin inscribed with the dealer's name. The worker with the nipped fingers always took good care not to emerge from the shop sucking them, for this did not elicit sympathy from other workers.

In the early eighteenth century, when the industry was booming, there were estimated to be over 100,000 lace workers throughout the country who earned over a total of £500,000 annually. This worked out at an average wage for each worker of approximately 2s. (10p) per week. A really good worker would earn up to 7s. (35p) a week, but out of this he or she would have to pay for thread, so the wage probably did not amount to more than 3 or 4 shillings (15 or 20 pence). At that time, however, these wages compared reasonably well with those of other skilled workers.

Seventy years later, however, the situation was very different, for the lace workers were living at near starvation level; the cost of living had risen considerably, but they were still earning only about 8d. (3p) per day.

William Cowper, the well known poet and friend of lace makers, tried to intervene on their behalf in Parliament, so moved was he by their plight. In the year 1780 he wrote:

> I am an eye witness of their poverty and do know that hundreds of this little town are upon the point of starving and that the most unremitting industry is but barely sufficient to keep them from it. There are nearly one thousand and two hundred lace-makers in this beggarly town.

Cowper was writing of Olney in Buckinghamshire. Other fair minded men were also beginning to be concerned about the welfare of the lace workers and one, Thomas Pennant, commented in 1783 that 'There was scarcely a door to be seen, during summer, in most of the towns, but what is occupied by some industrious pale-faced lass; their sedentary trade forbidding the rose to bloom in their sickly cheeks.' Others attributed the workers' ill-health to their working posture and the 'small close rooms in which many sit together.'

The lace makers' unhappy situation did not entirely escape the notice of the upper classes for in 1775, under the patronage of Queen Charlotte, two institutions (in Marylebone Lane and in James Street, Westminster) were opened in London for the purpose of 'employing the female infants of the poor in blond and black silk

lace-making and thread laces.' More than 300 children were employed, and the annual register states that, 'they gave such a proof of their capacity that many who had not been there more than six months carried home to their parents from 5s to 7s a month, with expectation of getting more as they improve.'

The hand lace-making industry started to revive in the early nineteenth century and the average daily earnings of each worker went up to about 1s. 6d. (7½p). This did not please the wealthier members of society who complained that lace making made women lace workers independent, and that female labour for domestic and agricultural work was scarce and expensive. When machine-made lace was introduced it virtually brought an end to the cottage lace industry. Earnings dropped disastrously to 6d. (2½p) a day.

Old workhouse records provide another fascinating glimpse into the lace industry. In the early part of the eighteenth century, when the lace industry was booming, workhouse inmates – who were traditionally employed on spinning and weaving – began instead to make bobbin lace. Since lace was a valuable commodity, strict rules and regulations were laid down to prevent anyone stealing a yard or two. Every piece of lace while still on the lace pillow was sealed at the ends. One workhouse regulation stated: 'If anyone in the Workhouse shall convey, take or steal lace belonging to the workhouse they shall be severely punished.' Another warned: 'If anyone in the workhouse shall convey, take or steal either ... lace or anything belonging to the Workhouse. ... They shall be punished as the law directs, with the utmost severity.'

Lace made in the local workhouses was normally sold for the benefit of the parish, and it realized about £30 a year on average. In 1743 the workhouses of Dublin made the magnificent sum of £160 by selling the bone lace made by the children. In Aylesbury in Buckinghamshire the overseers for the local workhouse recorded that they paid for '2 cloths for lace pillows and paid 4d to four girls for cutting off', and that a certain Mary Slade received '3s 7d to set up lace making'.

9 Children in The Industry

Probably the first mention of training children in the lace industry is in the overseer's count in the village of Eaton Socon in Bedfordshire in 1596 when an attempt was being made to make the poor of the parish self-supporting. Goodwife Clarke was paid 2d. (less than 1p) a week to teach each child how to make bone lace. The children were given the money they earned, but should the parents not send a child to learn they could get no parish relief. For this tuition Goodwife Clarke received 1s. (5p) for her first week of tuition. The original entry is shown in figure 14, and reads as follows:

> ijd the weeke to the woman that
> teacheth the pore children to worck
> bone lace. And every child thus
> worckinge shall weekly be paid from the
> gaine of Mr Beverly his stock so muche
> as they shal earne by their worckings;
> And such pore as doe not send their
> children being able to worck shall
> receive no relief from the collection.

At Woburn in Bedfordshire in 1618 the churchwardens were paying out sums ranging from 3s. (15p) to 7s. 6d. (37½p) for teaching the 'poore children' to make bone lace, and the Great Marlow Charity of 1629 made provision for teaching 24 women and children to make lace. Other workhouse accounts show that sometimes the workhouses apprenticed young girls to learn lace making until they were 16 to 18 years old. There are other overseer's accounts for the seventeenth century which show regular payments made to teaching the poor children of the parish to make lace, and for providing the necessary equipment.

The teachers were often inmates of the workhouse themselves, and were paid little for their services. A certain Jane Harris was paid only 1s. (5p) a week for her work in 1719, the same amount as Goodwife Clarke received over 120 years earlier. About 50 years later the payment crept up to 1s. 6d. (7½p), dropping back again 10 years later to 1s. (5p).

The most reliable information we have of children making lace comes from the lace schools, which seem to have started in the late eighteenth century. When the lace schools opened, children's charities dropped the practice of apprenticing girls to the lace trade. They discovered not only that 'health is frequently injured' and that in learning lace making 'little attention is paid to moral discipline and restraint', but also that 'girls who have been brought up to work at the lace schools, are generally found unfit for household work.'

Lace schools were common in all lace making districts, but there were many more in the Midland counties than in Devonshire. The Midlands had several lace schools in each village. The 'school', run by a lace mistress, was usually the sitting room of a small cottage which had poor heating, lighting, ventilation and sanitation. The more children she could pack in, the more money the lace mistress made for herself. There would often be from 20 to 30 children ranging in age from 5 to 15, both boys and girls, although boys left earlier to work on the land. The children sat in rows on stools while the mistress sat in front, usually with a cane on her lap.

It was normal practice to send children to the lace school at the age of five, and all the money they earned during the first year would be kept by the mistress in return for teaching them how to make lace. Sometimes a mother would teach a child at home for a year, and send him or her to the lace school at the age of six. In this way

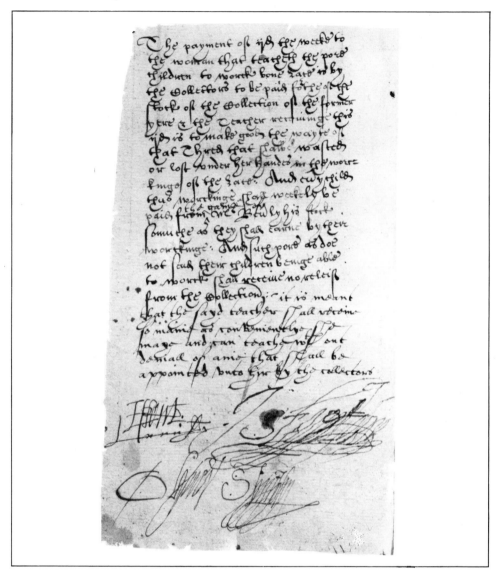

he or she earned money straight away, and suffered less at the hands of the mistress. A mother usually favoured her youngest child in this way, and he or she was often called the 'dilling'. It was probably much easier to teach the last child, too, since the older ones would already be at the lace school out of their mother's way.

After the first year the lace mistress would pay the children about 6d. (2½p) a week, which they got every month. Sometimes she would charge for her services, and in one particular school the fees were 2d. (a little under 1p) a week for girls and double that for the boys, because the boys

were double the trouble to teach.

One old lady recalled her grandmother saying, 'When I was five my mother took me to the lace school and gave the teacher a shilling. She learnt me for an hour, smacked my head six times and rubbed my nose on the pinheads.' The lace mistress could afford to lose no time in teaching the children for their work was money in her pocket. Even worse punishments were meted out, for in one school it was the custom to hang the boys up on a beam with a rope under their armpits, and to make the girls bend over their pillows while their bare necks were whacked with the cane. Indeed, it was the recognized custom that the little girls should always be dressed with arms and necks bare for easier slapping. One lace mistress complained that boys were a definite disadvantage in the schools because their arms and necks were covered, and their heads were too hard to smack.

The girls' hair was always neatly braided, lest a stray hair become woven into the lace, and they were not allowed to touch their faces or hair, for the lace had to be kept spotlessly clean. In some counties it was the practice to keep a bag of flour or dry starch next to the pillow to dry the hands and whiten the soiled lace; this was called 'getting up' the lace. In most lace schools, though, 'getting up' the lace was thought to be a shameful practice and any child found doing this would get a sharp smack and told to dry their hands on a cloth. There were always a few unscrupulous lace mistresses who would try and pass off dirty lace in this way rather than lose money.

In summer the children usually worked out of doors, and were required to empty a certain number of bobbins each day.

Thomas Wright, in his *Romance of the Lace Pillow* (1919), records that one lad solved his problem in a typically masculine way by winding the thread round and round the bole of a tree. The punishment he received is not recorded.

In one school the children were required to stick 600 pins an hour, and if they were five pins short at the end of a day they had to work an extra hour. Only those who have tried making lace will realize what a task this is, but in all schools some method was used to keep the children hard at work.

Some lace mistresses were more humane and did have the children's welfare at heart. They taught the children to read a little as well as make lace. Reading was usually from the Bible, and each child would take it in turn to read a verse out loud before beginning work in the mornings. Nevertheless, any levity or poor reading was frowned upon and earned an extra hour's work.

The children worked from 10 to 12 hours a day with a half-day on Saturday, and Sunday was always kept as a day of rest. The 12-hour day was normally

FIGURE 15
Left: fan edging; right: pea ring edging. Modern, made by a child. Children in lace schools began on these easy patterns

worked in summer when natural light was available and the 10-hour day in winter when candles were lighted. During the very infrequent breaks during the day the children were allowed to work on a 'play pillow' to do any lace edging they liked. Any money the children made by 'playing' they were allowed to keep for themselves. In the Midland counties the 'play' patterns were usually the 'ninepin', 'linen edge' and the 'pea ring' because they were simple and quick.

In winter, from November until February, the children worked by candlelight. They sat in a circle round a candle stool or candle block as shown in diagram 20 (top). This was a wooden stool about 30cm (2ft) high with a circle of holes round the outside and one in the middle. The middle hole had a socket which held a large tallow candle. By means of pegs and small holes the candle could be adjusted in height as it burned down. The outside holes held inverted water flasks, traditionally filled with 'snow water'. These flasks focussed the light onto the pillows as a magnifying glass would focus the sun's rays. The flasks rested on small rush rings called flash cushions. Rush baskets or 'hutches' containing the spare flasks hung on the candle stool. A tinder box for lighting the candle and a pair of candle snuffers were kept nearby.

The children sat on stools of varying heights. The highest stools were nearest the candle. There were usually two or three circles of children, the best lace makers sitting closest to the light and the others in the second or third circles, according to their merit.

Winter brought further hardships to the lace makers for they could not light fires to keep warm lest the smoke should soil the lace. In Normandy they worked over the cattle sheds in order to benefit from the warmth rising from the animals below. In England, particularly in the Midlands, the workers used 'fire pots', also called 'chad pots', 'dicky pots' or 'hot pots'. (See diagram 20, bottom.) These were about the size and shape of an old-fashioned chamber pot, usually made of rough brown earthenware, but also occasionally of iron or brass. Sometimes there was a

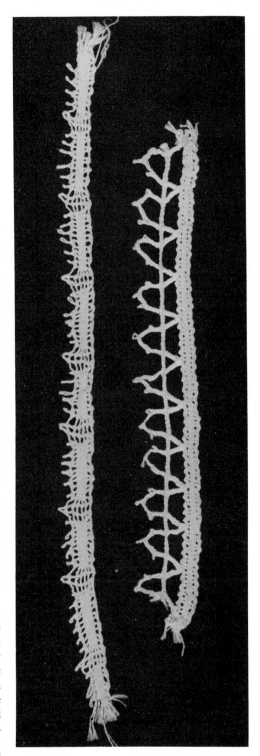

FIGURE 16
Left: Linen edge;   modern child.
right: ninepin edge. Practice pieces in old
Made by a young   lace schools

ring of small holes around the top for draught. They were filled with hot ashes bought from the local baker for a farthing on the way to work in the morning. The pot would normally keep hot for about half a day, after which it could be revived for the afternoon with a pair of bellows. The girls tucked the pots under their long skirts and occasionally a mishap would occur and a young lady would go up in smoke. The cry would go up, 'Somebody burns!', and the other girls would douse the smouldering petticoats with a bucket of water always kept handy for the purpose. Women who worked at home also used the pots and they would often take them to church on Sundays.

Holidays for the children were few and far between, but there were two very important feasts which all lace makers kept when young and old alike joined in the fun. These were St Andrew's Day on 30 November (Tanders) and St Cath-

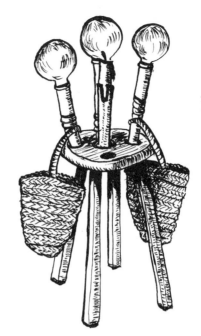

Diagram 20
Left: candle stool with straw hutches; above: hot pot, chad pot or dick pot

FIGURE 17
Flash or flask, and straw hutch for use on a candle stool. Reproduced by permission of Castle Museum, York

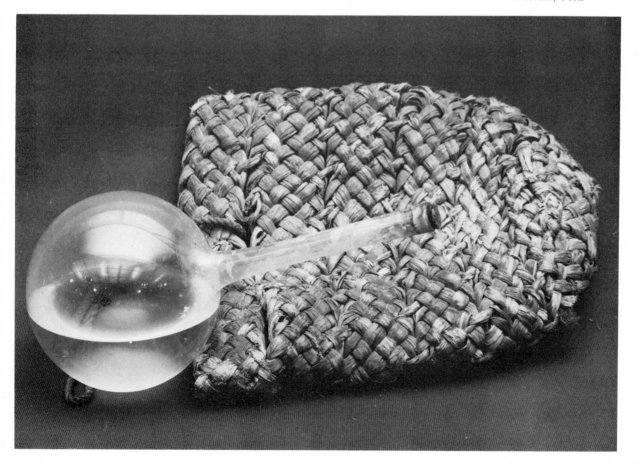

erine's Day on 25 November (Catterns). St Catherine was the patron saint of spinners, and lace makers considered that their craft was allied to spinning. There is a theory that Catterns was held in honour of Queen Catherine of Aragon, but there is no evidence to substantiate this.

On the holidays everyone ate, drank and made merry. Those who celebrated Tanders made a special dish called Frumenty (pronounced locally as 'thru-metty'). This was made by soaking new wheat, without the husks, in the oven for a day until it was soft and jellied, and then adding hot milk, plums, cinnamon, sugar and nutmeg. Hot metheglin was drunk with it. This was an alcoholic drink similar to mead and was made of honey, sugar, malt and spices fermented with yeast. Tanders cake was another delicacy. It was probably a type of bread since the base was bread dough to which lard, sugar and caraway seed was added. Caraway seed was an important ingredient in many of the special holiday dishes.

Each village had its own way of celebrating Tanders. In one village the women made sweets called 'black buttons', and in another the villagers always received a gift of figs from a local gentleman since his birthday fell on St Andrew's Day.

The evening of Tanders was the time for the young to indulge in riotous games, dancing and singing. A traditional game was 'bite the apple'. A thread holder from a bobbin winder was suspended from a beam, a piece of apple was spiked on two of the blades and a piece of tallow on the other two. The victim was blindfolded and invited to take a bite. Biting the tallow caused much merriment. If the children had a pleasant lace mistress she would join in the fun as well. The children would lock her out of the room, and sing:

> *Pardon, Mistress, pardon Master*
> *Pardon for a pin*
> *If you won't give us a holiday*
> *We won't let you in!*

Catterns was celebrated in much the same way as Tanders. Cattern cakes were made with dough and caraway seeds. In some villages the girls were roused early by the local bellman calling out:

> *Rise, maids rise!*
> *Bake your Cattern pies*
> *Bake enough, and bake no waste,*
> *And let the bellman have a taste.*

The dish eaten at the feast in the evening was stuffed, baked rabbit covered with a thick onion sauce. In Wendover in Buckinghamshire the lace makers called Catterns 'candle day' because it was the day they lit the candles at the start of winter. They made a round, sponge gingerbread cake, again flavoured with caraway seeds which they called 'wigs', apparently because the edges of the cake curled up like those of a wig.

The Catterns drink was warm beer thickened with rum and beaten eggs. A favourite game for the young on Cattern's night was jumping over the huge candlestick. The lace-makers used these large candlesticks as well as the candle stools, and they were all of 60cm (2ft) tall. The following rhyme was chanted as the girls and boys joined hands and danced round it:

> *Wallflowers, wallflowers, growing up so high*
> *All young maidens surely have to die;*
> *Excepting Betsy Turvey, she's the best of all*
> *She can dance and she can skip, and*
> *She can jump over the candlestick.*
> *Turn, turn, turn your face to the wall again.*

Then Betsy, having accomplished the difficult task of jumping over the candlestick without putting out the flame, would face outwards from the circle. The game was over when all had faced out towards the wall.

Children today sing another version of this old rhyme beginning:

> *Wally, wally wallflower*
> *Growing up so high,*
> *We will all marry, we will all die.*

The children of Suffolk, and probably other counties, sing the following as they jump over skittles:

> *Jack be nimble, Jack be quick*
> *Jack jump over the candlestick!*

Suffolk was once a lace making county, although it never had a large scale lace industry.

These games were widespread, with

slight local variations. In Ireland for instance, the idea was to put out the candle flame with the tip of the toe, without touching the candle or the candlestick.

A few villages kept other days as holidays as well as, or instead of, the two great feast days. Shrove Tuesday was a half-day holiday, and the great attraction on this day was the pancake race. Olney in Buckinghamshire is still famous for its pancake race. Other minor holidays were St Thomas's Day on 21 December, May Day on 1 May and, in the village of Cranfield in Bedfordshire, 5 November and 14 February were holidays, these being the days on which the lace makers began and ended working by candlelight.

By the end of the nineteenth century most of the old customs had died out with the decline of the lace industry.

Lace schools also thrived in Europe, for there is an early mention of a school in Flanders by a certain Andrew Yarranton, a gentleman of London, in the year 1677. In a tract entitled *England's Improvement by Sea and Land, to outdo the Dutch without Fighting* he wrote:

Joining to this spinning school is one for maids weaving bone lace, and in all the towns there are schools according to the bigness and multitude of the children. I will show you how they are governed. First, there is a large room, and in the middle thereof a little box like a pulpit. Second there are benches built about the room as they are in our playhouses. And in the box in the middle of the room the grand mistress, with a long white wand in her hand. If she observes any of them idle she reaches them a tap, and if that will not do, she rings a bell, which, by a little cord, is attached to the box. She points out the offender, and she is taken into another room and chastised. And I believe that this way of ordering the young women in Germany is one great cause that the German women have so little twit-twat and I am sure it will be as well were it so in England.

Another contemporary account of lace schools comes from Cooke in his *Topography* of Devon. He wrote:

The sallow complexion, the weakly frame and the general appearance of langour and debility of the operatives are sad and decisive proofs of the pernicious nature of the employment. The small unwholesome rooms in which numbers of these females, especially during their apprenticeship, are crowded together are great aggravations of the evil.

In the nineteenth century some effort was made to improve the working conditions of the young people. In 1843 the Commissioners on the Employment of Children laid down that the hours the children worked should be graded according to age, the youngest children working four or five hours each day, the hours rising with age until the young women were working 12 to 15 hours a day, which were in any case very long hours compared to our eight-hour day. In Devon the height of the lace pillow was raised to prevent children stooping all day. Sanitation was generally improved. Mrs Palliser, in her *History of Lace*, first published in 1875, mentioned that she visited a lace school, and commented: 'The children looked ruddy as the apples in their native orchards', and that a girl lace maker was 'more healthy than the female operatives in our Northern manufactures.' She regretted, though, that children were not allowed to 'march and stretch their limbs at the expiration of every hour.'

From the mid-nineteenth century there were many health, welfare and education Acts which put so much pressure on the lace schools that many were forced to close. Some parish schools still went on teaching lace making during the second half of the nineteenth century, although it was discouraged by Education Authorities.

At the beginning of the twentieth century, lace making was still a livelihood for a number of workers. The North Bucks Lace Association, for instance, employed some 300 workers, and opened lace schools for children. There was, however, no real hope of hand-made lace manufacture ever surviving as an industry as by then machine-made lace could be produced far more cheaply and quickly.

10 The Lace Tells

Long hours spent sitting over a lace pillow were not only unhealthy, but also boring, especially when yard after yard of the same lace pattern was produced. To make the time pass more quickly and pleasantly, the girls chanted 'tells' or 'tellings', which were rhymes said in a sing-song voice.

Many of them were spine-chilling tales of corpses, shrouds, coffins and murders. This is not surprising for each town, village or hamlet had its own blood-curdling ghost or hobgoblin legend; many of them are still told in the villages today. Other tells were more cheerful and romantic, concerning weddings, lovers and romances. In the English lace counties, the Buckinghamshire tells are said to be the most gruesome, while the Bedfordshire and Northamptonshire ones tend to be more romantic.

The lace tells are like nursery rhymes in that they have been handed down from generation to generation by word of mouth and their origins never really known. The women of the lace districts remember the tells their mothers or grandmothers taught them, even though they are not lace makers themselves. Apart from slight variations from county to county the tells are basically the same. Many of them have been adapted by children as skipping rhymes.

Perhaps the earliest reference to the lace tell is that in Shakespeare's *Twelfth Night*, when Duke Orsino says, 'O fellow, come, the song we had last night. Mark it, Cesario, it is old and plain. The spinsters and the knitters in the sun, and the free maids that weave their threads with bones, do use to chant it.'

From this reference it appears that other workers besides lace makers also chanted tells. The word 'free' in this context means 'without care'.

Other countries also had their own tells. In Saxony (Germany) the girls sang of the 'Twelve geese who stole the oats' and the 'Cuckoo with thirty wives'.

Tells with a great many repetitive verses were very popular.

Sometimes the tell was not a rhyme but simply a calling out of the amount of work to be done such as:

19 miles have I to go
18 miles I have to go,

and so on.

The number 19 crops up frequently in the tells, probably because this was often the number at which the work was started.

The following tell is one of the gruesome ones in which a girl tells of how her scheming lover tried to murder her. She arranged to meet him in a wood at night and when she arrived early she found him already there digging her grave by lantern light with the help of a friend. In the tell she calls him the 'Fox'.

Nineteen miles as I sat high
Looking for one and two passed by,
I saw them that never saw me –
I saw the lantern tied to a tree.

The boughs did bend and the leaves did shake
I saw the hole the Fox did make
The Fox did look, the Fox did see,
I saw the hole to bury me!

This old Buckinghamshire tell contains another little murder plot. The last lines refer to the practice of calling out when every 50 or 100 pins had been stuck in the pillow, each girl trying to be the first to call out to prove her skill. The 'rod' in line two was to whip her with.

Get to the field by one
Gather the rod by two

Tie it up at three,
Send it home by four,
Make her work hard at five,
Give her supper at six,
Send her to bed at seven,
Cover her up at eight,
Throw her down the stairs at nine,
Break her neck at ten,
Get her to the well lid by eleven,
Stamp her in at twelve.
How can I make the clock strike one,
Unless you tell me how many you've done?

Occasionally the lace worker, perhaps when she was behind with her work, was forbidden to talk to anyone for a given length of time. This was called a 'glum' or 'time of gloom'. The 'glum' ended when a required amount of pins had been stuck. More often all the girls were silent together and if one dared to speak before the communal glum was up another glum was imposed on the talker. These periods of self imposed silence gave the girls an opportunity to concentrate on the work in hand so that they could get ahead. In the following tell the silent spell was set for 31 pins. If anyone looked up from her work or spoke, the penalty was another 31 pins of silence!

Dingle dangle, farthing candle,
Put you in the stinking dog's hole
For thirty-one, speak or be silent for sixty-two!

Another tell which required a glum of eight pins takes the form of a conversation between two workers:

Knock, knock at your door.
Who's there?
It's me.
Come in.
Does your little dog bite?
Yes.
How many teeth has it?
Six; seven next time; eight when I call again.

At the end of a glum everybody relaxed again and chanted:

Tip and stitch and turn over,
Let it be hay or let it be clover,
For my glum's done.

This lace tell comes from Bedfordshire, where lace makers are considered to make splendid wives:

Come all you bold batchelors merry and free,
If you want to live happy be ruled by me;
If you want to live happy all the days of your
  life,
You must take a lace maker to be your sweet
  wife.
Lace makers rise early in the morning betimes,
And do their odd jobs before the sun shines,
And then they sit down to their pillows
  complete,
I love to see lace makers work it so neat.
They all get together in the sunshiny day
Their pillows are shine like the blossoms in
  May.
Their fingers are lissom, their bobbins are
  small,
And now I have told you the truth of it all.
The great servant girl, she runs down in the
  hall,
Great holes in her stockings, no shoes on at all;
Great holes in her clothes, scarce a rag to her
  back,
To take a lace maker is all that I lack.

This one is a variation on the above theme:

Up in the morning, before it is light,
Done all her work before it is bright,
Down at her pillow she sits so complete
Like a lace maker, working so neat,
With fingers so lissom, and bobbins so small,
While the poor servant girl goes down to the
  hall,
With holes in her stockings and rags on her
  back.
I'll be a lace maker, if ever so slack,
I'll turn over timber sticks,
  Put in my pin of wire,
My wire pin is in,
  I'm the one nigher.

The following tell is the story of a beautiful Bedfordshire maiden who was rescued from the unwelcome attentions of a highwayman by a stalwart Bedfordshire farmer. This obviously comes from the eighteenth century because of the mention of the highwayman.

In Bedfordshire lived a rich farmer, we hear;
A Bedfordshire maiden had lived there a year,
She started for home a short holiday,
When a highwayman stopped her upon the

highway,
She screamed out with fright, she screamed out
with fear,
But help ('twas the Bedfordshire farmer) was
near,
The highwayman, hit by the blunderbuss, died;
And there soon was a wedding and she was a
bride.

This lace tell comes from Kempston in Bedfordshire, and was chanted in the lace schools of the mid-nineteenth century to the tune of: soh, soh, soh, doh, doh, doh, ray, me, ray, doh. As each line was chanted a pin was stuck, and after the whole had been chanted beginning with, 'Nineteen long lines . . .', it was repeated again, beginning with 'Eighteen . . .' and so on till the last line began, 'No long lines . . .'. There are 35 lines in the tell, so that at the end a total of 700 pins had been stuck.

Nineteen long lines hanging over my door,
The faster I work it will shorten my score.
And when I do play it will stand at my stay,
So my little fingers must twink it away
For after tomorrow comes my wedding day.

My shoes are to borrow, my husband to seek,
So I cannot get married till after next week,
And after next week it will be all I care
To pick and to curl, and to do up my hair.

Six pretty maidens, so neat and so clean,
Shall dance at my wedding next Monday
morning.
Down in the kitchen the cook she will run
And tell Mr Bellman to ring the ting-tang.

I'll tell father, when father comes home.
What a day's work my mother has done.
She's earned a penny, she's spent a crown,
She's burned a great hole in her holiday gown.
She's earned a penny, she's spent a groat,
She's burned a great hole in her holiday coat.
Father came home in any angry fit
And swore a pottle loaf should last us a week!
He cut himself hunches, and me little bits:
I all the time wonder at his naughty tricks,
Father whipped mother, and mother whipped
me,
They was such a racket, you seldom do see,
Then mother she sent me a long way from
home,
She sent me to go by the beats of the drum

The beats of the drum and sweet music did play
For that was my grandmother's grand wedding
day.
The miller was driving his waggon along,
The trees were in blossom, the nuts looked so
brown.
They hang so ripe, they won't come down,
Let's fetch hooks, and hook them down.
Who'll buy plums, I'll buy flour,
And we'll have a pudding in half an hour.

Any suitable names could be inserted in the jingles; the name in this one was also changed to suit the whim of the moment:

Up the street and down the street
With windows made of glass;
Call at Polly Perkins door –
There's a pretty lass!
With a posy in her bosom,
And a dimple in her chin;
Come, all you lads and lasses,
And let this fair maid in.

The above tell is reputed to belong to Bedfordshire, but an old lady whose family hailed from Dorsetshire said that her grandmother taught her the tell when she was young. Her grandmother was a lace maker, so the tell must have been widely known.

For a worker who failed to maintain silence during a glum, another punishment was in store:

Hang her up for half an hour
Cut her down just like a flower.

An indignant protest from the culprit would run:

I won't be hung for half an hour,
I won't be cut down like a flower.

Many people will recognise part of an old popular nursery rhyme in the following tell:

Nineteen miles to Charing Cross,
To see a black man ride on a white horse.
The rogue was so saucy he wouldn't come
down,
To show me the road to the nearest town
I picked up a turnip and cracked his old crown,
And made him cry turnips all over the town.

Sometimes the girls amused themselves by playing a game called 'Round and

Round the Town' or 'Up and Down the Parish'. In this game each worker had to call out the name of a person living in the village until everyone had been accounted for. It could be varied endlessly by calling out the names of all the girls in the village, followed by the boys' names, and so on.

One can find many different versions of most of the tells, which is not surprising, since they have been handed down by word of mouth and have often suffered through not being written down. Two old sisters trying to recall a tell gave the author two different versions, after much argument, and they had both learnt it from their mother. Usually, however, the basic story or meaning of the tell is not altered, it is simply a question of each village, county or lace school adding a piece of local dialect or colour to the original version.

Many people will remember the old nursery rhyme, 'I had a little nut tree . . .'. There were two slightly different versions of this in the lace making world:

I had a little nutting tree
And nothing would it bear,
But little silver nutmegs
For Galligolden fair.

The word 'nutting' is used in Devon, while in other areas 'nut tree' is more common. What the silver nutmeg is we are not sure, but *gilt* or *gilded nutmegs* are referred to as long ago as the seventeenth century. Some lace makers say that the silver nutmeg refers to a container for pins.

Another familiar nursery rhyme crops up in the following tell:

A lad down at Weston looked over the wall,
And saw nineteen little golden girls playing at
*   ball.*
Golden girls, golden girls, will you be mine?
You shall neither wash dishes nor yet feed the
*   swine*
But sit on a cushion and sew a fine seam,
Eat white bread and butter and strawberries
*   and cream.*

Sometimes it ends: 'And eat nothing but strawberries and sugar and cream.' 'Golden girls' was the special name given to the footside pins in lace making, because of the gold wax pin heads.

Another special name for a particular pin occurs in this tell. It is the 'striver' pin, which is referred to as the 'old lady'. These pins were important because they were the markers indicating how swiftly the work was proceeding, or how skilful the worker was.

Needle pin, needle pin, stitch upon stitch,
Work the old lady out of the ditch,
If she is not out as soon as I
A rap on the knuckles will come by and by
A horse to carry my lady about
Must not look off till twenty are out.

There is little doubt as to what punishment was in store for the child who slacked and did not get her 20 pins out in time.

This jingle from Northamptonshire trips merrily off the tongue:

Twenty pins have I to do,
Let ways be ever so dirty
Never a penny in my purse
But farthings five and thirty.

Mary Letts and Alice Betts
They are two bonny lasses
They built a bower upon the tower
And covered it with rushes.

The following tell reflects the anxiety to get the allotted amount of work completed before dark in the winter, for it was no fun working by candlelight:

Nineteen miles to the Isle of Wight,
Shall I get there by candle light?
Yes if your fingers be nimble and light
You'll get there by candle light.

This tell mentioned below is very interesting, for it found its way to Canada, and was sent back to Britain by a correspondent of the *Bedfordshire Times* at the turn of the century. Judging from the date he gave, it must have originated in about 1830:

The Clarke of the parish you know very well
Gets up in the morn to ring the eight o'clock bell
He being so handy with his pipe and his pot,
To lock the church doors, he really forgot.
The mare and the foal went in at full speed,
Got hold of the Bible, and began for to read.
Stop, stop, said the foal, before you begin,
You shall be parson, and I'll say Amen.
We preach about tailors, and they are no men,
For they cabbage the cloth, and sell it again.

I wish to my heart the thimble had a hole
To prick their old fingers, Amen said the foal.
We preach about bakers, who bake all the
  bread,
And that would not matter if they were all
  dead,
For they inch it and skinch it, and roll it and
  roll,
Until the devil can't part it, Amen said the
  foal.
Next we preach about brewers, who brew all
the beer,
Then buy the malt cheap, and sell the beer dear.
A very good thing if the copper had a hole
To run all the beer out, Amen said the foal.
Last, we preach about blacksmiths, and they
  are jolly men,
For they pull the old shoes off and shoe them
  again.
We wish to our hearts that the anvil and hole,
Was its own weight in gold, Amen said the
  foal.

11 Equipment for Making Bobbin Lace

The lace pillow

Lace pillows varied in shape and size according to tradition and the type of lace being made. There were 'round' pillows (see diagram 21, top), which were really bolster shape with open ends, and 'square' pillows (see diagram 21, bottom), which did not really look square because of the rounded corners. These types were popular in the East Midland counties. A 'French' pillow had a small revolving bolster set in a padded frame on which the bobbins rested (see diagram 22, bottom). It could only be used for very narrow edgings, but it was convenient because the parchment could be pinned right round it and 'setting up' was avoided. The French pillow was seldom used in England; in fact, the English workers scathingly called it a 'drawing-room pillow'. A 'Belgian' or 'Bruges' pillow was circular. It was often referred to as a 'half mushroom' (see diagram 22, centre). Devon workers also used this type of pillow because it could be turned round easily, a necessity when making the detached motifs for Honiton or Brussels lace. A 'Spanish' or 'Maltese' pillow (see diagram 22, top) was a long bolster shape with one narrow end which

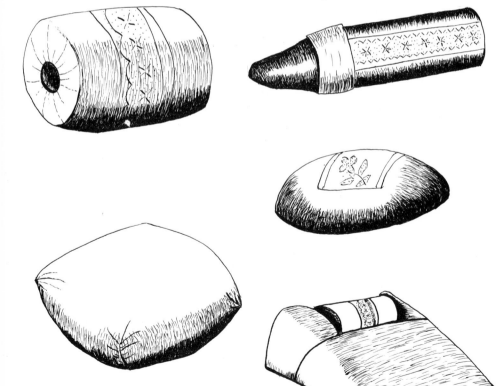

Diagram 21
Top: round pillow;
bottom: square pillow

Diagram 22
Top: Maltese pillow;
centre: mushroom or
Belgian pillow;
bottom: French
pillow

FIGURE 18
Patricia Payne, lace teacher, working on her pillow resting on a bowed horse

was called a 'pillow cloth'. After the parchment was pinned to the pillow, a cloth known as a 'worker' was pinned over the bottom half of the parchment to take the friction of the bobbins and another, known as a 'drawter', was pinned over the top half. The 'drawter' was also used to fold over the completed lace which was wound round a 'lace card', and held in place by a cardboard 'tucker'. A further cloth called a 'heller' was used to cover the whole pillow when not in use.

Pillow horse or maid

Some of the round and square pillows were bulky and heavy, and a special stand was needed to support the pillow. It was called a 'pillow horse' or a 'maid'. It was wooden, and usually made by the local village wheelwright or carpenter. The early type, shown in diagram 23 and known as a 'single horse', was a simple three-legged stand with a bar across the top on which to rest a pillow. A further development was the 'bowed horse', shown in diagram 24, which had a curved bar on the top forming a semi-circle, into which the pillow rested and required no further support. Later a collapsible horse, shown in diagram 25, was invented. All of these horses had a stretcher bar across the front on which the worker rested her feet. Italian pillows sometimes had a table stand and, at the end of the nineteenth century, a box stand for bolster pillows was sold. The Bruges pillow was sometimes sold mounted on wood with a drawer underneath.

Pins

Pins were of prime importance to the lace maker. Brass pins which did not rust were used. They were longer than normal and came in several different thicknesses. The lace makers called them 'long toms' or 'yellow pins'. Until the seventeenth century pins were imported from France and were very expensive, so many of the early lace makers improvised by using long thorns. (This is interesting, for Dr Johnson says that the word 'pin' is derived from the Latin work 'spina' which means 'thorn'.) In Devonshire the thrifty sea-faring folk

was gripped between the knees while the other end was rested against a table or chair back. The lace was worked down the pillow, not round it.

The pillow was usually made of canvas or similar strong material, which was then stuffed with wheat straw (see figure 18). The straw was chopped into 15cm (6in.) lengths and then hammered down hard in the pillow with a wooden mallet. This was very important if the pillow was to remain hard. The old workers insisted on the pins 'pinging' when put into the pillow, otherwise the pillow was not considered satisfactory. Straw in the bolster-shaped pillows was packed longitudinally.

The pillow was covered with a piece of material, usually of butcher blue, which

Diagram 23
Single horse (earliest type)

Diagram 24
Bowed horse (adjustable)

Diagram 25
Collapsible horse (latest type)

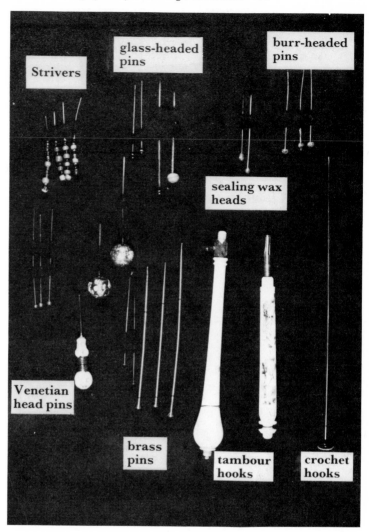

FIGURE 19
Selection of pins, prickers and hooks

used fish bones, sharpening and cutting them to a regular size.

Pins with solid heads did not come into general use until about 1830. The early pins had separate heads of fine twisted wire which were secured to the shanks by compression with a block and die. They were not very efficient as the heads frequently fell off in use.

The lace makers often decorated their pins by slipping a few coloured beads on to the shank and securing them with the head from another pin. They called these pins 'limicks', 'king pins' or 'bugles'. An ornamented pin was also called a 'striver' because the worker would time herself to see how long it took her to work the pin out. Sometimes the seed of goose-grass,

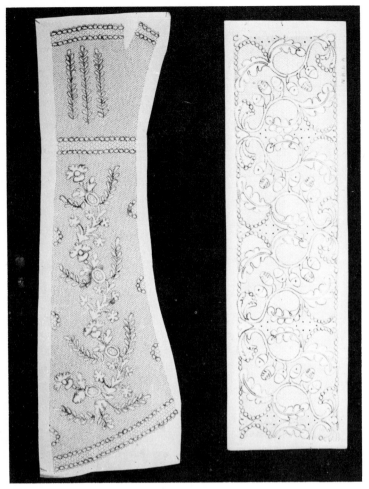

bobbins; a small pair of scissors and a chain and, occasionally, a flour bag.

A 'needlepin' was a special tool used by Devonshire workers to join parts of their lace pattern together. This was a very fine needle set into a small wooden handle. Sometimes a very fine crochet hook was used instead.

Coloured pins were not really necessary for identification. They appear to have been used to enhance the lace pillow. The latter must have been a most attractive and cheerful sight with its spangled bobbins and coloured pins, especially on dull, grey days.

Before we finally leave pins, it is interesting to note the following advertisement which was printed on the old fashioned pin paper when new one-piece pins were made:

> The inimitable patent Solid Headed Pins exclusively made by D F Tayler and Co London on a new and improved principle, are unlike those of any other manufacturer in consequence of the whole pin being formed of one piece of wire, whereby the head is rendered immovable and its slipping off is impossible.

Parchments

The old lace patterns were called 'parchments' because they were actually pricked on to parchment. The men who designed the lace patterns were great artists, and it is to these early designers that we owe many of the beautiful designs of machine-made lace today.

A designer would prick his first draft on card or vellum, and ink in the essential design of the pattern as well as any gimp lines. He also inked in tallies, connecting bars and any other such features. He normally pricked only one repeating element of the design.

The lace dealers would supply the workers with the drafts or 'cards' as they called them, and the workers would usually prick their own parchments. Sometimes, however, the parchments were pricked by someone specially employed for this purpose, as we know that the trade of

known as 'burhead' or 'sweetheart', was slipped on to the pin. This soon became polished with use and looked most attractive. Another way of decorating the pins was to put blobs of red or gold wax on the heads. The red pins were usually put on the headside of the lace and the golden ones on the footside. Pins with bone heads, decorated or inscribed in the same way as the bobbins, were occasionally used. These are collectors' items now.

Extra long pins, called 'corking pins', were used for fastening the parchment pincushion or bobbin bag to the pillow. Putting the cloths on the pillow was called 'dressing the pillow', but the latter was not completely dressed without a pin cushion stuffed with bran, the slight oiliness of which kept the pins from rusting; a bobbin bag with compartments for full and empty

'parchment pricking' is referred to in old documents. The pricking was done over a lead sheet simply called a 'lead'. When a lead became badly pitted it was melted down and re-used. (That is probably why very few are in existence today.) Later the pricking was done over thick felt pads.

To transfer a pattern to a pricking, transparent parchment was spread over the draft, and pricked and inked in the same way as the draft. This pricking needed absolute precision for if it was the tiniest fraction of an inch out, the whole pattern would be thrown out of line.

Each parchment was usually 35cm (14in.) long, and this was called a 'down', for when the worker reached the bottom of the parchment she took all her pins out and moved her work up to the top again. The latter was referred to as 'setting up',

and was a tedious business. At the end of the parchment, cloth tabs were sewn to fasten in onto the pillow. These tabs were called 'eches', a name probably derived from the word 'eke' i.e. to spread out.

The old lace makers treasured their parchments, and, when asked where these came from, they would say, 'Oh, but we always had the cards.' A theory is that many of the old cards were originally brought from the continent by the refugee lace makers. Today glazed cardboard has replaced parchment for pricking patterns.

The original tool for pricking parchments was made of brass, but later an awl was used, or a steel needle forced into a bobbin or a wooden handle. Sometimes a blob of sealing wax was stuck on the end. More sophisticated tools had turned wooden handles and a screw device so that

FIGURE 21
Sample prickings for Beds-Maltese lace and Bucks ...nt lace. Reproduced by permission of Luton Museum and Art Gallery, Luton

the point could be changed. All that was really required, however, was an implement with a sharp fine point and something to grip it with.

Thread

In the heyday of lace making every type of thread imaginable was used to produce lace: linen, cotton, wool, silk, gold and silver thread, even human hair. In Le Puy, France, lace was made at one time from the hair of goats and angora rabbits. Lace made of human hair was probably only a passing fashion for the finished product was not durable and would frizzle up under heat. It was called *point tresse*. There is in the Northamptonshire Museum a sample pattern book which has a specimen of this hair lace.

In England the best and most durable lace was made from pure linen thread, imported from the continent and costing as much as £200 for 450g (1lb.). As each lace maker bought her own thread, this could be quite a heavy expense although the lace manufactured from a pound of thread could be sold for more than £600. The thread was sold in skeins, which were numbered according to the fineness of the thread. The higher the number, the finer the thread; 300 was very fine. Until the end of the eighteenth century the thread was spun by hand, but then machinery took over. Hand-spun thread was recognizable because it was joined approximately every 50cm (20in.), this being the distance a spinner could comfortably reach from her distaff.

In the early nineteenth century cotton thread was used widely in England. It was called 'gassed thread' because it had been drawn through a gas flame to remove loose fluff. It was generally considered inferior to linen thread but was cheaper. It also had the advantage of being more elastic and of breaking less easily. Most industries eventually used Scottish cotton, except for making Alençon and the finer pieces of Brussels, Mechlin and Valenciennes. The cotton thread was sold in 'parcels', each parcel containing a number of 'slips'. The more slips, the finer the thread. The thread used for Brussels lace was extra-ordinarily fine, and was made from flax which was cultivated especially for the purpose.

It was impossible to make this ultra fine thread in any other country, so the art of making true Brussels lace remained exclusively in Flanders, to the considerable financial benefit of that country, for during the eighteenth century an ounce of lace was worth approximately ten times more than an ounce of gold. In 1787, for instance, 450g (1lb.) of flax was sufficient to make lace worth over £700. In 1859 the same weight of Brussels thread was sold for £500.

Woollen thread was also used to make lace. Originally the thread was supposed to have been made from yak's hair, but in England it was usually made from woollen thread derived from Yorkshire sheep. Woollen lace was made in the Midland counties of England from about 1870.

Natural silk lace was called 'blond' lace, and was made in England from the mid-eighteenth century. Silk lace thread came in black, white and cream.

Gold and silver laces were always popular with the rich, especially for use on state occasions. Gold thread lace was made in the East Midland counties at the end of the nineteenth century, but the workers disliked making it because of its tendency to curl on the pillow; 'twipper up' was the local expression. Gold thread was imported into England from Cyprus, until the sixteenth century, when Turkish intervention prevented the English from trading in the Mediterranean. Venice then took over as the key trading centre for gold thread, and supplied Europe with 'Venice Gold', to replace 'Cyprus Gold'. It was extremely expensive. The Coopers' Company was paying 54s. (£2.70) for 540g (1lb.) of it in 1565. As we saw in an earlier chapter, the Venetians often sold poor thread or gave short measure to the anger of the English who protested that:

They bare the gold out of this land
And sowkethe the thrifte out of our
  hands
As the waspe sowkethe the honey of the
  be.

In 1565 English craftsmen mastered the

FIGURE 22
Antique bobbin
winder with solid
wheel and egg-cup
bobbin holder

art of manufacturing metal threads by a method imported from Nuremburg in Germany. Until then it had been necessary to send gold and silver to Germany to be made into thread. The new English-made thread was called 'sewing gold'. It was still expensive: 28g (1oz) cost 5s. (25p) in 1572. Such was the demand for the new thread that James I, with an eye to making a quick fortune, sold patents to members of the Wire-Drawers' Company, and the skeins of gold thread were sealed with each maker's own mark. Profiteers then began to make inferior thread, as a result of which the Wire-Drawers' Company registered the mark of each of its members so that inferior threads could be traced.

Bobbin winders

Every lace maker liked to own her own bobbin winder which she sometimes called a 'turn'. It saved her a considerable amount of time because otherwise all her bobbins would have to have been wound by hand.

The traditional bobbin winder was made of wood. It consisted of a base, which sometimes contained a drawer for bobbins, and a large grooved flywheel with a handle. A small leather belt or cord turned a pulley round which turned an egg-cup-shaped bobbin holder. Also fixed to the base was a skein holder with adjustable pegs to take the thread. The thread was given a couple of turns round the neck of the bobbin, and the spangled end of the bobbin was held in the bobbin holder with the left hand. The thread was also guided with the left hand, while the right hand was used to turn the wheel.

All flywheels and bobbin winders were

FIGURE 23
Mahogany spoke
wheel bobbin winder
with skein holder

basically the same, varying only in small details of construction or decoration. Later bobbin winders were designed to be clamped to a table, but they worked on the same principle as the earlier ones, except that they needed a separate skein holder.

Lighting equipment

The use of the candle stool or candle block in lace schools has been explained in Chapter 9, but the home lace maker had to provide her own lighting as best she could. If she could afford it she would buy an oil lamp or a lace maker's lamp which resembled an ordinary candle stick but had a glass sphere instead of a candle holder. The sphere had a small hole in the top so that it could be filled with water. A candle was then placed behind it so that

the sphere magnified the candlelight. These lamps were manufactured from the 1780s to the 1850s. They can still be found in antique shops but they are now very expensive.

Many lace makers could not afford these lamps, so they improvised by using the sphere only, or even a bottle of suitable shape, turned upside down and placed in a container. The spheres or bottles were traditionally filled with snow water, probably because snow water was soft and would leave no scale on the glass.

Other equipment

There were other pieces of equipment which a lace maker might have, not all of which were essential.

A small pair of scissors was always kept

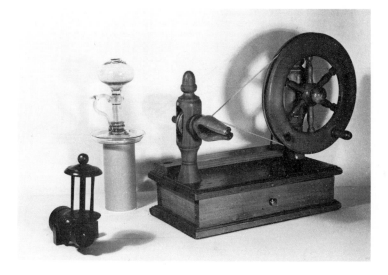

hanging by a chain or cord either on the pillow or on the worker's belt.

A bobbin box, often made by the men folk, was another item often found in a lace maker's home. It was used for spare bobbins, and usually had two compartments, one for large bobbins and one for the small long-necked bobbins.

Even the poorest cottage usually had an oak lace chest with two compartments: a large one on top to take the lace pillow, and underneath it a drawer (or drawers) to take the bobbins and other equipment.

A yard-stick or yard-wand was used on cutting off days to measure the lace. A simple length of wood marked off in inches with notches or brass nails served this purpose adequately.

A lace drying bottle, a simple round bottle covered in flannel, was another essential piece of equipment. The lace was stitched to the flannel and immersed in soapy water. It was then gently washed and rinsed by hand and the bottle then inverted over a stick in the garden to dry. The sunlight and air bleached the lace.

FIGURE 24
Right: Deal bobbin winder with spoke wheel; centre: lacemaker's glass lamp; left: separate skein holder

12 Bobbins

Bobbins, no matter how beautiful or elaborately decorated, served a purely functional purpose. A plain bobbin did the job just as well as a fancy one. Its purpose was to act as a spool on which to wind the thread, and to provide a means of manipulating the thread while keeping the required tension. An elaborate piece of lace would require up to 1,000 bobbins.

Over the centuries bobbins changed in shape and design but the most remarkable and highly decorated bobbins come from the English Midland counties. Some of the earliest bobbins still in existence are of Flemish origin. They are plain with a knob at the top on which to wind the thread, and a bulbous base for weight and tension. Gradually bobbins began to get slimmer and more attractive until, by the end of the eighteenth century, they were seldom thicker than a pencil, and were about 8 to 10cm ($3\frac{1}{2}$ to 4in.) long without the spangle. There were thicker, heavier and longer bobbins, specially designed for heavy thread such as yak or worsted wool, metal threads or gimp.

Early bobbins were made of small animal bones. Hence in early wardrobe accounts and other old documents bobbin or pillow lace is referred to as bone lace. Later, bobbins were made of many different materials, but wood or bone were the most popular because these were cheap and readily available. Wood bobbins were probably first made in Bedfordshire. The wood normally used was close-grained, dark hard wood or fruit wood, such as cherry, plum, apple, damson, maple, walnut, blackthorn, yew, spindlewood or bog-oak. For bone bobbins any suitable animal bones were used. Sometimes special souvenir bobbins were made from bones saved from a joint at a wedding or funeral feast.

Ivory, ebony, brass, pewter, silver, gold and glass have all been used to make bobbins. Glass, silver or gold bobbins were made only for presentation purposes, glass being too fragile, and gold and silver too expensive, for practical use. These are extremely rare now, and a collector is lucky to find one. Since brass is a very heavy metal, bobbins made of this had to be slim. Pewter was not popular because, apart from being expensive, it was very soft and easily bent out of shape in use. Ivory bobbins were unknown in England, but they were made in India and in other countries where missionaries attempted to teach the natives lace making. These are also collectors' items.

Bobbin making was a trade in its own right, and in the heyday of lace making many bobbin makers were established in England. The bobbin maker would travel from village to village selling his wares. He always carried a stock of bobbins inscribed with popular Christian names, romantic texts and simple decorations. The more elaborate and personal bobbins were made to order, and delivered on his following visit, or they could be ordered and collected at the village shop. Cheap, colourful, gaudy bobbins were sold at fairs and were called 'fairings'.

The bobbin maker used a lathe driven by a foot pedal to turn the bobbins. There is on record a bobbin maker who used a water-powered lathe to turn his bobbins. He always charged more for bone bobbins than for wooden ones. Since, however, the bone bobbins lasted much longer than the wooden variety, they were the best purchase in the long run. Great ingenuity was shown in decorating the bobbins, and the lace makers were equally inventive in naming them.

Every bobbin maker had his own

method of making coloured dyes and of applying them. Wooden bobbins took dye unsatisfactorily, and few are now in existence. Some of the mottled ones were light wood dyed with aqua fortis (nitric acid) but the dyeing process was seldom successful. Bone bobbins took colour very well, and the natural colour of the bone enhanced the dyes. Coloured bands, spots and inscriptions were achieved by dying the whole bobbin and then turning it on the lathe again to remove the surface colour, the spots or bands having been drilled or cut first. Another method was to mix the colour with gum arabic, and then work it into the dots by twirling with a crow quill.

The pewter 'leopards' had holes drilled right through the shank which were then plugged with pewter. 'Tigers' (pewter stripes) and 'butterflies' (wing-shaped strips of pewter) were made by cutting grooves in the shanks, putting them into a stone mould, and then running in molten pewter. All the surplus pewter was then trimmed off to surface level.

The 'church window' or 'mother-in-babe' bobbins were made by soaking the larger bobbins until they were pliable and then squeezing in the baby bobbins. When dry the larger bobbins contracted, holding the babies in place.

All brass-bound bobbins had grooves cut to take the wire so that it lay level with the surface.

Archibald Abbott, a Bedford bobbin maker, always stamped his name on the shank, and coloured his bone bobbins red by boiling them in a solution of log-wood chips. It is rare now to find an Abbott bobbin and worth searching for if you are a collector. (See figure 25(5).)

The following is a summary of the different types of English bobbins. There are, however, bobbins in existence which do not fit into any given group. Many of them are unique, having been adapted from continental bobbins, or hand whittled.

Wooden bobbins

Dumps or **bobtails** were wooden bobbins without spangles. They were smaller in length and thickness than an ordinary

FIGURE 25
(1) Hand whittled bobbin; (2) Leopard; (3) Butterfly; (4) Tiger; (5) 'ABBOTT' bobbin name at bottom of shank; (6) Pewter banded and named 'ANN'

FIGURE 26
Wooden bobbins: *Top row left to right*:
(1) Old maid cowrie spangle and bone heart; (2) Baluster turned; (3) Baluster turned, bird cage spangle; (4) Bitted;
(5) Spliced;
(6) Tiger;
(7) Butterfly;
(8) Leopard;
(9) Inscribed 'WILLIAM' (10) Tallie (11) Mottled.
Bottom row left to right:
(12) Yak; (13) Cow-in-calf; (14) Cow-in-calf; (15) Mother-in-babe (probably Indian);
(16) Mother-in-babe;
(17) Wired;
(18) Trolly, pewter gingles; (19) Gold thread. Reproduced by permission of Luton Museum and Art Gallery, Luton

bobbin. An early type of bobbin, they were used for very fine lace where heavier bobbins would have broken the thread. Some of these bobbins were later drilled and spangled.

Thumpers were bulbous bobbins without spangles, mainly found in the High Wycombe area of Buckinghamshire. (See figure 29.)

Plain turned bobbins are shown in figure 27. The extra thin ones were known as **'old maids'**.

Ornamental turned bobbins included varieties such as **baluster**, **ball-and-reel**, etc. A selection of these, showing the great artistic skill of the lathe turner, are shown in figure 27.

Grooved turned bobbins were formed by a sharp tool being held against the shank while it was being turned. This resulted in a series of small grooves around the shank.

Pewter inlaid bobbins were of three main types. Those inlaid with rings of pewter were called **Bedfordshire tigers**; those with spots were called **Bedfordshire leopards**; and the ones with a splayed pattern in the form of insects' wings were known as **butterflies**. There were also miscellaneous pewter inlaid designs following no set pattern.

Spliced bobbins were made by two different coloured woods being spliced together, usually diagonally. Sometimes wood-and-bone were spliced and, rarely, metal-riveted. Splicing was also a method of repairing bobbins.

Coloured or **mottled bobbins** were decorated either with grooved coloured bands or with patches of colour.

Sectional bobbins were composed, as their name implies, of sections of light and dark coloured woods.

Bitted bobbins were nearly always wooden with a different coloured wood inlay in various designs. Very occasionally a bone inlay can be found.

Tallies were usually wooden with a broad pewter band (sometimes 2½cm, 1in., wide) let into the shank. They were given this name because they were used to carry the thread for working the tallies, or plaits, on point ground. Sometimes a name or an inscription might be punched into the pewter band, but this is rare because the

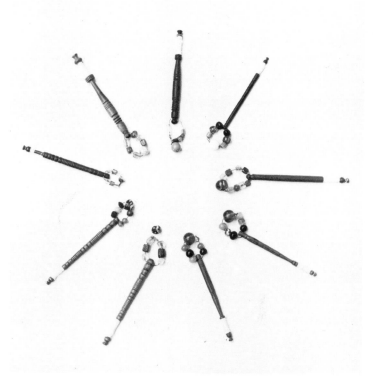

FIGURE 27
Selection of turned wooden bobbins

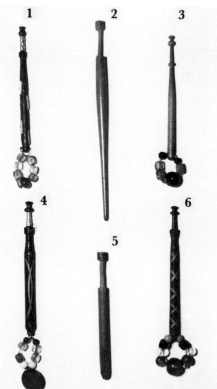

1 **2** **3**

4

5

6

FIGURE 28
Selection of wood and bone bobbins:
(1) Old maid;
(2) School pen and pencil whittle to make bobbin; (3) Bitted, wood and bone;
(4) Bitted; (5) Hand whittled; (6) Bitted

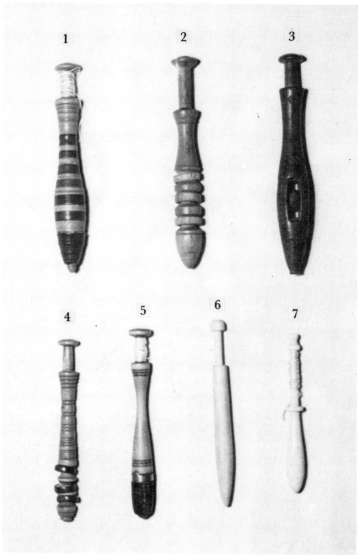

FIGURE 29
Selection of wood and
bone bobbins:
(1) Thumper South
Bucks bobbin;
(2) Trolly South
Bucks bobbin;
(3) Thumper South
Bucks bobbin;
(4) Trolly South
Bucks bobbin;
(5) Thumper South
Bucks bobbin;
(6) Downton bobbin;
(7) Child's bone
bobbin

pewter wore away quickly and the inscription disappeared.

Big wooden bobbins

Metal thread bobbins were large with a single neck which formed a spool to hold gold or silver thread.

Yak bobbins were large and heavy to take woollen thread for worsted lace.

Ouills were never used on the lace pillow, but used to wind on a skein of gimp thread which was rewound on to trolly bobbins for the pillow.

Trollies, also known as **trailers**, were slightly bulbous, very strong and had several loose pewter rings called 'gingles'. Bone trolly bobbins are rare, especially those which have bone rings instead of pewter. Also rare is a wooden bobbin with wooden gingles. A trolly bobbin carried the gimps which outline the pattern on net grounds.

Bone bobbins (see figure 30)

Bone bobbins could be plain or ornamental, and were turned in exactly the same way as wooden ones. They also had similar pewter inlays. Since they took colour better than wooden ones, the whole bobbin was dyed, usually red or green, though blue or mauve were also fairly common.

Domino bobbins had tiny drilled holes filled with colours such as red, dark blue or black. They also had coloured grooved bands, indentations and fancy marks.

FIGURE 30
Bone bobbins: *Top row left to right*:
(1) Baluster turned;
(2) Incised decoration;
(3) Wired; (4) Wired bone spangle;
(5) Tinsel; (6) Wire beaded; (7) Wire beaded; (8) Butterfly;
(9) Leopard;
(10) Tiger;
Bottom row left to right:
(11) Wired inscribed 'JAMES'; (12) Trolly: bird cage spangle;
(13) Mother-in-babe;
(14) Mother-in-babe;
(15) Mother-in-babe: bird cage spangle;
(16) Bird cage;
(17) Inscribed 'JOSEPH CASTLE HUNG 1860';
(18) Inscribed 'SARAH HOBBS DIED FEB 10TH 1836 AGED 18 YEARS';
(19) Inscribed 'ACCEPT THIS TRIFEL FROM A FRIEND WHOSE LOVE TO THEE WILL NEVER END'.
Reproduced by permission of Luton Museum and Art Gallery, Luton

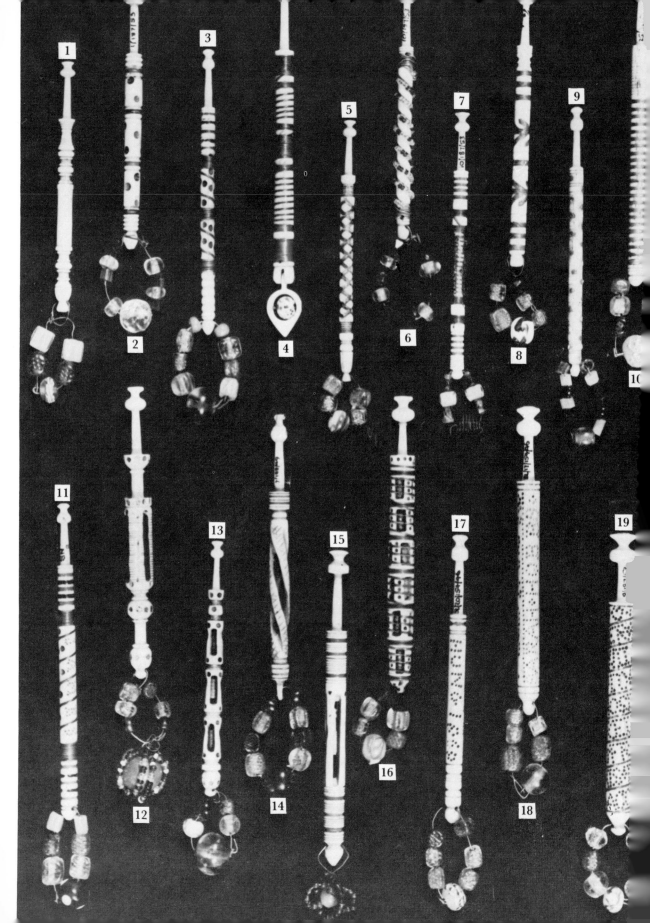

FIGURE 31
Selection of wood and
bone bobbins:
(1) Spliced, bone and
wood, named
'KATHARINE';
(2) Tunbridge ware;
(3) Baluster, bone,
stained green;
(4) Purple and gold,
bone; (5) Domino;
(6) Spliced wood
bound with wire

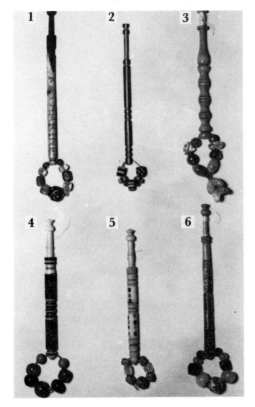

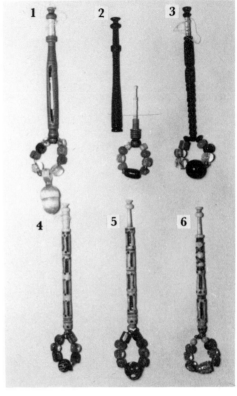

FIGURE 32
Selection of bobbins
made from various
materials: (1) Beaded
bird cage; (2) Beads
forming shank;
(3) Tinselled;
(4) Pewter bands
inscribed 'MY DEAR
LOVER'; (5) Ivory
beads; (6) Domino
and wired

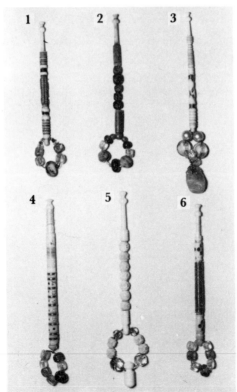

FIGURE 33
Selection of mother-
in-babe style bobbins:
(1) Mother-in-babe;
(2) Cow-in-calf;
(3) Church window;
(4) Mother-in-babe;
(5) Mother-in-babe;
(6) Mother-in-babe

Bound bobbins were bone or wood, bound with brass wire placed in specially cut grooves so that it remained level with the surface. Sometimes the wire was bound tightly round the whole of the shank.

Wire and beaded bobbins had tiny beads threaded on brass wire and wound round the shank in spirals or patterns in grooves in the same way as the plain wire. Occasionally the whole shank was covered in this way but few of these examples have survived because of their fragility. Bound and inscribed bobbins are extremely rare.

Tinsel bobbins were sometimes known as **fairings** because they were sold at fairs. With red, blue, green or gold tinsel set in spirals in grooves, they were very gaudy. (See figure 32(3).)

Mother-in-babe bobbins, also called **church windows**, shown in figure 33, were made by the shank of the bobbin being hollowed out and vertical slits cut, the whole effect being of tall church windows. As many as 12 windows can be found on a bone bobbin, but four is the usual number on a wooden one. In each compartment there was usually a tiny bobbin, but lead shot, wooden beads, glass beads or little balls of wire were not uncommon. It would be difficult today to find a bobbin with several windows and all the baby bobbins intact.

Bird-cage bobbins were cut similarly to the **church windows** but bound round with brass wire to resemble the bars of a cage. The wire prevented the miniature bobbin from falling out. A different **bird-cage** was made by making the bobbins in two horizontal halves, and joining it together by upright wires threaded with little beads, thus making a cage in the centre. (See figure 32(1).)

Cow-in-calf bobbins, also known as **jack-in-the-box bobbins**, were made in two sections, one fitting tightly into the other. The inside of the shank was hollow and contained a miniature bobbin. Sometimes the small bobbin was joined on to the base of the top section. If made of brass, the two sections sometimes screw together. It is unusual today to find the baby bobbin inside, unless fixed.

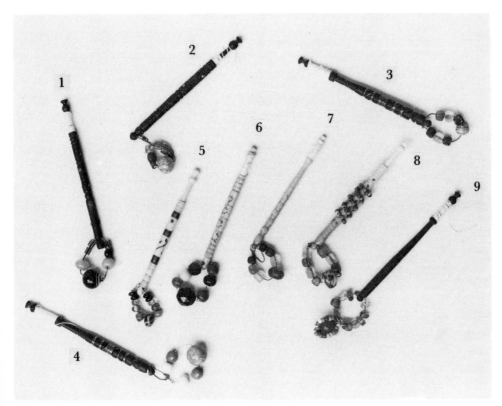

FIGURE 34
Selection of bobbins:
(1) Bedfordshire leopard;
(2) Bedfordshire leopard; (3) Wood wire bound;
(4) Wood wire bound; (5) Bone wire bound incised red/blue spots;
(6) Bone engraved 'LUCY'; (7) Bone bound; (8) Bone beaded with incised spots; (9) Wood turned, bird cage spangle

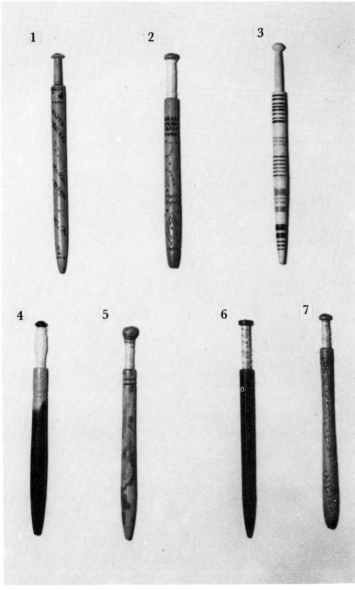

FIGURE 35
Branscombe and
Honiton bobbins:
(1) Honiton bobbin
inscribed 'COME UP
LITTLE HORSE WILL YOU
BUY ANY FISH, ONE FOR A
PENNY TWO FOR A KISS';
(2) Honiton bobbin
inscribed 'HEARTS AND
FISH'; (3) Branscombe
bobbin; (4), (5), (6)
and (7) Honiton
bobbins

Devonshire, Wiltshire and Dorsetshire bobbins

The typical Devonshire bobbins have no
spangles because of the technique of
'sewing' used in Honiton and Brussels lace
making. These Devonshire bobbins have
pointed ends.

There were two kinds, **Honiton lace
sticks** and **trolly bobbins**. The latter were
not the same as the Midland **trollies**.
They were so called because they were
used to make Devonshire trolly lace and

had blunt ends.

The **lace sticks** were usually made of
spindle-wood, olive-wood or mahogany.
The bobbins were decorated simply in
comparison with the Midland bobbins.
Quite often they were incised, but never
drilled. They carried designs with a
nautical flavour, such as fishes, anchors,
seaweed and ships, reflecting Devon's
close ties with the sea. The designs were
usually stained black and red, and sometimes carried inscriptions. Wiltshire bobbins were similar to Devonshire bobbins,
but were slightly thicker and shorter, as
were the Dorsetshire bobbins.

Whittled bobbins

This was the name given to bobbins which
had been carved by hand rather than
turned on a lathe. Some were beautifully
carved, and were obviously a labour of
love, while others were crude, roughly cut,
utilitarian bobbins. Nearly all of these
bobbins were made of wood, but very
occasionally one would be made of bone.
Sometimes wooden bobbins were decorated with poker burns, and the spangle
holes were not drilled but burnt through
with hot wire. Inscribed bobbins are dealt
with in the following chapter.

Spangles

The purpose of the spangle, or circle of
beads attached to the bottom of the
bobbin, was to add a little weight to the
bobbin in order to give the thread tension
and to stop the bobbin rolling around on
the lace pillow when not actually in use.

The beads of the spangle were specially
designed and used only for lace-making
bobbins. They were small and square,
usually white or red in colour, although
shades of green, blue and amber were
occasionally used. They were threaded on
brass wire.

The beads were made by melting a stick
of glass and pressing the sides with a file
while hot. This roughened the sides and
'squared' the bead. These beads were
traditionally called **square cuts**. The mark
of the file could clearly be seen on
authentic beads. As diagram 26 shows,

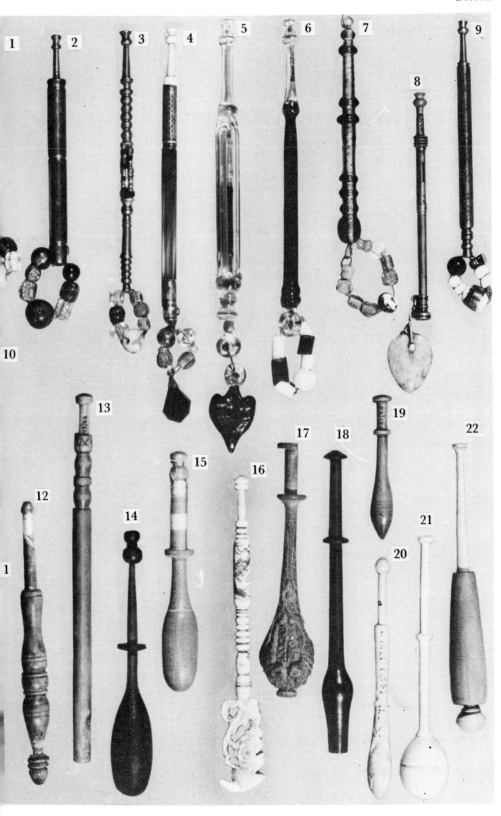

FIGURE 36
Selection of bobbins
from all over the
world: *Top row left to
right*: (1) Pewter
mother-in-babe;
(2) Brass mother-in-
babe; (3) Brass bird
cage; (4) Agate
shank; (5) Glass
mother-in-babe;
(6) Glass; (7) Glass;
(8) Silver pencil
holder, Breccia
marble spangle;
(9) Brass inscribed
'MERCY LOVE'; *Bottom
row left to right*: (10)
and (11) two Honiton
bobbins, top one
dated 1807;
(12) Maltese;
(13) Russian
(Vologda); (14) French;
(15) Modern French
with horn protector;
(16) Indian (East
Midlands type);
(17) Burmese
inscribed 'AKYAB
1900'; (18) Belgian or
Flemish; (19) French
Valenciennes;
(20) St. Helena name
inscribed;
(21) Portuguese;
(22) Austrian with
wooden protector.
Reproduced by
permission of the
Luton Museum and
Art Gallery, Luton

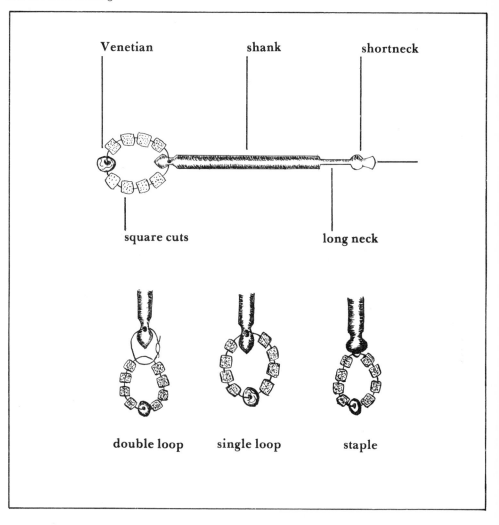

Diagram 26
Top: parts of a
bobbin; bottom:
methods of fixing
spangles

there were normally nine beads on the spangle, four square cuts on each side and a large Venetian bead on the bottom. The Venetian beads were sometimes called **pompadours**, and they were round. The lace makers usually bought the square cuts separately and wired them themselves. Quite often the bottom bead was replaced with mementoes or tokens. Buttons, coins, shells, lockets, crucifixes or lucky charms were all used.

Many of the bottom beads were beautiful. Some were opaque with tiny coloured scrolls; others were transparent, and coloured designs could be seen through them. One type of bottom bead, much sought after by collectors, is called **Kitty Fisher's eye**, and was named after a very beautiful eighteenth century actress. The

bead was larger than usual, and grey in colour. It had small circular dots of white on it, with a small blue dot in the centre. Sometimes the centre dot is red.

The **bird-cage spangle** was also interesting. This consisted of a large bead surrounded by a cage of tiny beads threaded on wire. It is unusual to find one today since the wire is easily broken and the tiny beads lost.

Spangles were attached to bobbins in two ways. They were either threaded directly through a hole drilled in the bobbin shank, or looped through a circle of wire which was then put through the shank. Sometimes a staple was put into a bobbin to take a spangle, but it was not a good method of attachment because the staple soon worked loose and fell out.

13 Inscribed Bobbins

Inscribed bobbins are the most fascinating from the collector's point of view. Many bobbins have the same inscriptions but with different spellings. Occasionally the bobbin maker put in an extra letter or two, or left some out, either by mistake or through lack of space, or else because he just could not spell. Far more bone bobbins were inscribed than wooden ones, because the inscriptions quickly wore off the latter. Bone bobbins carried the most interesting inscriptions. The inscriptions were added by drilling tiny holes into the bobbin and filling them with black, red or dark blue colouring. Capital letters were almost invariably used for the inscriptions; it is very rare to find any other form of lettering. They were either drilled horizontally along the length of the bobbin or spirally around it. If the bobbin was too short to take all the words on one line, the remaining words were drilled in a second line underneath the first. To read a spiral inscription you need to rotate the bobbin while you hold the head away from you and the spangle towards you. The inscription can then be read from the bottom up or, more usually, from the top down. It is unusual to find a bobbin with a carved inscription. If you do, it will be a bone bobbin, probably carved with a single name or word. Misspelt words were fairly common, as were unevenly spaced letters. A collector should look for these eccentricities. Spaces left between words often had a dot in the space, or perhaps four dots, spaced thus ·.·.

There are many thousands of inscribed bobbins still in existence, but they may for convenience be grouped under a dozen major headings according to the type of inscription they bear. All the inscriptions quoted below are on bobbins which are now in museums, or private collections, or which have been authentically recorded.

Names, dates, origins, family ties and occupations

Most dated bobbins are from the nineteenth century. Bobbins inscribed with dates earlier than this are therefore comparatively rare and collector's items.

The most common inscriptions were Christian names because personalized bobbins made welcome presents, just as inscribed pens or pencils do today. Almost all the old-fashioned Christian names, both men's and women's, were represented, e.g. LUCY, PHEBE, CHARITY, ARON, JOB. Some have alternative letters in different colours to make them more interesting. Christian names with a date added were much less common, e.g. 'MARY 1822'. Christian names and surnames together were usual, e.g. 'REBECCA BATES'; often a date was added as well, i.e. 'ANN WOOLASTON 1821'.

Names and villages were fairly common; occasionally they go in family sets, e.g. 'WILLIAM, JOSHUA, ELIZABETH AND MARY WAITE, YARDLEY HASTINGS'. An inscription with the name of a village and county in full was very unusual, and only a few exist.

Christian names were sometimes preceded by the words 'DEAR', 'SWEET' or 'LOVELY', e.g. 'SWEET WILLIAM', but these were fairly rare. Relationships were also included in some inscriptions, such as 'DEAR FATHER', 'MY DEAR SISTER 1870' and 'MY SON HABRAM PRENTIS'.

Bobbins inscribed with names and occupations are very rare. Luton Museum has in its collection one wooden mother-in-babe bobbin inscribed 'WILLIAM CLARK SHEPORD GOOD GAL MAKE CAST AND WORK' (William Clarke, Shepherd, good girl, make haste and work) which is unique. Another example in existence is 'THOMAS BARKER BRADFIELD GREEN SWEEP'. Thomas Barker was a sweep and a lacemaker from Brayfield, Northampton.

Gifts and presents

Bobbins given as presents or gifts were very common. The inscriptions on these follow a fairly predictable pattern: e.g. 'A NEW YEARS GIFT FROM A FRIEND', 'A PRESENT FROM MY AUNT 1842', 'FOR BETSY'. Sometimes bobbins were given by the lace mistress to a good pupil, and occasionally a lace dealer would give one to a good worker. There are a number of bobbins still in existence inscribed 'THOMAS LESTER' or 'A PRESENT FROM THOMAS LESTER'. Thomas Lester was a very well-known Bedford lace dealer and designer who rewarded workers in this way.

Love, courtship and marriage

The best group of inscriptions are those dealing with love, courtship and marriage. The girls sitting for long hours over their lace pillows no doubt dreamt of their lovers and prospective husbands, while the men working in the fields would think of their sweethearts working on their lace. Typical inscriptions of this kind were: 'MERCY LOVE' (see figure 36(9)); 'IF MY LOVER LOVES IT IS TRUE HE WILL BE' (see figure 37(5)); 'LOVE DONT BE CROSS'; 'LOVE BUY THE RING' and 'I WANTS A HUSBAND' (the last three shown in figure 38(1), (3) and (4)).

The lads would give the bobbins as love tokens to the girls. If a boy was too shy to give it to the girl personally, he would get someone else to put it on his lady-love's lace pillow at night so that she found it the next day.

In this group can also be included those bobbins with inscriptions which refer to soldiers and sailors. Some begged the boys not to enlist, e.g. 'DON LIST LOVE' (don't enlist love), others recorded a joyful return home from sea, e.g. 'JACK ALIVE'. Sometimes one can find a bobbin with a soldier's button on the spangle.

Political, historical and national events

Another group of bobbin inscriptions are those recording historical events, such as 'WATERLOO 1818' and expressions of patriotism, e.g. 'QUEEN CAROLINE FOR EVER'. Those recording national events are still fairly plentiful, while those commemorating local happenings are harder to find. Similarly, bobbins inscribed with the names of national politicians and elections are more common than those commemorating purely local figures and elections.

Religious texts and sentiments

Religious texts were frequently inscribed on bobbins for lace makers were God-fearing people who strictly observed the Sabbath. Many of them were chapel goers. Texts such as 'JESES WEPT', 'LOVE JESUS', 'THE LORD WILL PROVIDE', were very common. Sets of bobbins each with a phrase or two of the Lord's Prayer were made, but few remain and it is a lucky collector who finds a complete set.

Family memorials

Memorial bobbins usually recorded births or deaths, e.g. SARAH HOBBS DIED FEB 10 1836 AGED 18 (see figure 30). Sets of bobbins can be found which commemorated the births or deaths of a married couple, a whole family, the children of one family. Examples of the last are the bobbins inscribed to commemorate the births of the Setchill triplets, Faith, Hope and Charity, born on 10 June 1831.

As mentioned already, memorial bobbins were sometimes made from suitable bones taken from the meal at a wedding breakfast or birthday dinner.

Violent deaths

Bobbins commemorating violent deaths such as murder, suicide and hanging were rare. As far as we know, bobbins were inscribed to commemorate only six executions and one suicide. That does not mean that only one of each was inscribed, but that bobbins were inscribed to commemorate only those seven events. Because the bobbins are rare and much sought after, a little of each story is given under the names of the people involved.

Matthias and William Lilley 1829

These two young men, aged 29 and 21 respectively, were poaching in a wood when a gamekeeper called King caught them. For some inexplicable reason the gun they were carrying went off and King accused them of attempted murder. They were sentenced to death, and hanged on Biddenham Gallows just outside Bedford Jail on 4 April 1829. Their grief-stricken mother lived for only four more years. She was buried at Kempstone, and there are three names on her tombstone: her own and those of Matthias and William. There are only a few bobbins commemorating this event in existence.

Sarah Dazeley 1843

Twenty-two year old Sarah Dazeley was convicted of poisoning her second husband, William Dazeley, with arsenic. She had married him only five months after the death of her first husband, Simon Mead. Sarah said at her trial that William Dazeley had poisoned her nine-month-old baby girl and then poisoned himself. She was found guilty of William's murder and the court suspected that she had also poisoned her first husband. She was hanged on 5 August 1843 at Bedford. William was buried in Wrestlingworth, Bedfordshire, the village where he died.

Joseph Castle 1860

Castle's wife was found on 9 August 1859 behind a hedge near Luton with her throat cut. Castle, a 24-year-old malt-maker had disappeared. After a bloodhound at Luton police station had tracked him down, he was brought to trial at Bedfordshire Assizes where he pleaded not guilty, saying his wife had cut her own throat after a quarrel. He was found guilty and sentenced to a public hanging on 31 March 1860. He confessed on the way to the scaffold. The evening after the execution, his wife's friends held a party and

each guest was given an inscribed bobbin (see figure 30[17]). There was probably quite a number of these bobbins, although there is no record of the number of guests at the party.

Franz Muller 1864

This murder of bank clerk Thomas Briggs by Franz Muller raised national interest because it was the first murder to be committed on a railway train. As a result of the ensuing public outcry railway officials eventually installed the communication cord system for emergencies.

Thomas Briggs was travelling from Fenchurch Street Station to his home in Hackney, London, when he was attacked and robbed by Muller who, after taking his gold watch and chain, pushed him out of the train and left him for dead. Briggs was, in fact, still alive but he died the following day. The blood-stained compartment aroused suspicion. Muller was caught after he had exchanged Briggs's gold watch chain for a new one at a jeweller's. The jeweller put the new chain in a box with Muller's name on it. Muller later gave the box to a child, and the child's father took it to the police. By this time Muller was on his way to New York on a sailing vessel. The police overtook the sailing ship in a steam ship, and brought Muller back to England. He was tried at the Old Bailey, found guilty, and hanged at Newgate. Muller confessed before he died.

William Worsley 1868

William Worsley was tried jointly with Levi Welch at Bedfordshire Assizes for the murder of William Bradbury of Luton. Welch turned King's Evidence and was pardoned, but Worsley was executed on 31 March 1868. As this was the last public hanging in Bedford, there was a considerable number of bobbins inscribed for souvenirs. These are, therefore, easier to obtain than the other execution bobbins (see figures 37(6)).

Welch was later brought to trial for robbing the murdered man, was found guilty, and sentenced to 14 years' penal servitude. He was, however, released after three months, having successfully pleaded

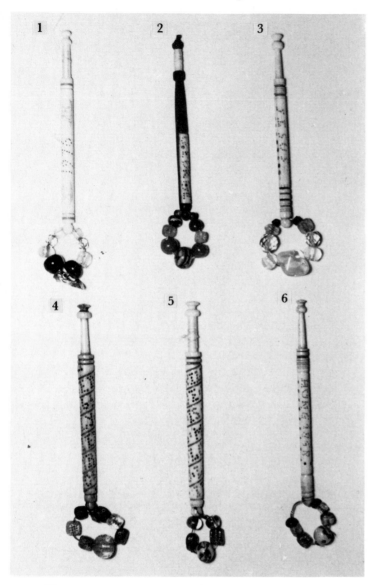

FIGURE 37
Selection of inscribed
bobbins: (1) Modern
commemorative
bobbin; (2) Bitted
bone on wood, named
'GEORGE';
(3) Inscribed 'JESUS
WEPT'; (4) Inscribed
'THOS KIMBLE DIED JULY
6TH 1865 AGED 70';
(5) Inscribed 'IF MY
LOVER LOVES IT IS TRUE
HE WILL BE';
(6) Hanging bobbin
inscribed 'WILLIAM
WORSLEY HUNG 1868'

that he had won a free pardon by turning
King's Evidence for the murder.

William Bull 1871

William Bull was hanged for the particularly vicious murder of Sarah Marshall
(nicknamed 'Old Sally'), a simple old lady
who lived by herself in a single-storey
tumble-down cottage in Bedfordshire. She
was the subject of much teasing and
tormenting by the local men and the children. Bull, one of her chief tormentors,
was also a heavy drinker. On the night of
29 November 1870, after a heavy bout of
drinking, Bull murdered the old lady in a
savage attack. For this motiveless murder
he was hanged on 3 April 1871. Although
the hanging was not public, the local
people were so incensed by the crime that
they gathered in Bedford on execution
day, and the pedlars made a considerable
amount of money by selling inscribed
bobbins as souvenirs. There are a number
of these still in existence.

There were also reputed to have been
bobbins inscribed with the name of Bull's
victim, Sarah Marshall. Thomas Wright,
in *Romance of the Lace Pillow*, claimed that
he had seen one owned by a Dr Lulham of
Stonehouse, Gloucester. However, there is
some controversy as to whether or not
these bobbins existed at all, and any
serious collector should make careful
enquiries before accepting one as authentic. If an authentic bobbin inscribed
with Sarah Marshall's name were found, it
would be very valuable as a collector's
item.

Joseph West

Joseph West hanged himself in the lock-up
at Cranfield, Bedfordshire. He was confined for some minor misdemeanour, possibly drunkenness, for one night, but the
next day he was found hanged 'with a
bootlace'. A bobbin commemorating this
event would be rare.

Richard Dillingom

Richard Dillingom was transported to
Botany Bay in Australia for theft. His
crime was probably minor; had it been
sheep stealing, he would have been hung.
Bobbins commemorating this event are

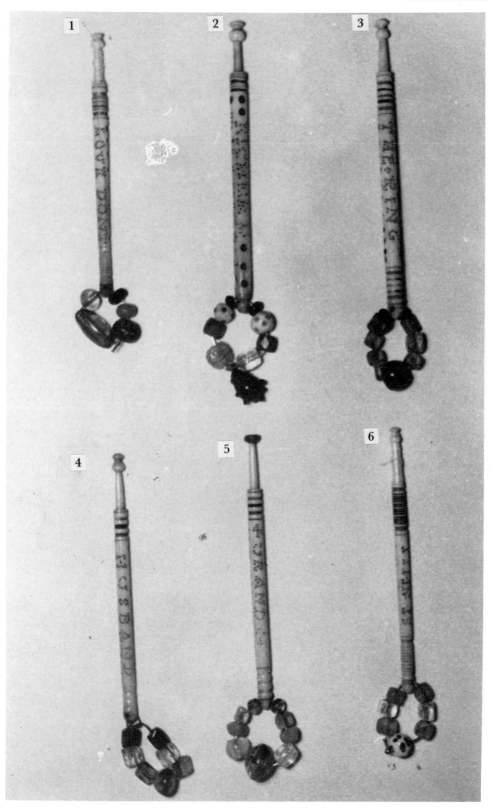

FIGURE 38
Selection of inscribed
bobbins:
(1) Inscribed 'LOVE
DONT BE CROSS';
(2) Inscribed
'RICHARD DILLINGOM AT
BOTANY BAY';
(3) Inscribed 'LOVE
BUY THE RING';
(4) Inscribed 'I WANTS
A HUSBAND';
(5) Inscribed 'X U R
AND X U B AND XX U R TO
ME'; (6) Inscribed
'TIME IS SHORT'

also collectors items (see figure 38(2)). This bobbin is recorded by Thomas Wright as being inscribed 'Rannson Dillinghum', but this is probably due to a combination of an inscription that is difficult to read and poor spelling on the part of the inscriber.

A collection of inscriptions

The following are examples of inscriptions on bobbins. Christian names are so numerous that only a few unusual ones are given. All the inscriptions on bobbins were in capital letters.

Christian Names
MERCY, PRISCILLA, AMELIA, BENJAMIN, FAITH, HOPE, ENOCH ELIZAR

Christian Names and Dates
MM 1816   CY 1861 LU

Full Names and Dates
ELIZAR JUFCUT 1833
TIMBROSE FELLS 1858
KEBLIB RANBOW FEBRUARY 5 1883
ANN PENEY 1812
MR JOHN BUTCHER TC 1831

Names, Places, Dates
THOMAS EMBERTON
THOMAS ROBINS   HARTWELL
SARAH BERREL BOZET   HAGED 8
PAUL GARDNER   BUGBROOK
WILLIAM PETETT   AMPTHILL
JOHN MALLET   MY DEAR RIDGEMOUNT
HENRY ASH   LITTLE HORWOOD 1840

Prefixed, and Relationship
DEAR UNCLE
ANN HULL MY DEAR AUNT 1865
LOVELY THOMAS
DEAR BETSY

Gifts and Presents
A PRESENT FOR MISTRESS BRIDE
A CHRISTMAS BOX
KEEP THIS FOR MY SAKE DARLING
ACCEPT THIS TRIFEL FROM A FRIEND WHO
   LOVE TO THEE WILL NEVER END.
A KEEPSAKE
A NEW YEARS GIFT 1861
WHEN YOU SEE THIS REMEMBER ME IN
YOUR MIND FOR ALL THE WORLD IS
NOUGHT TO ME AS LONG AS YOU ARE
KIND
WHEN YOU SEE THIS REMEMBER ME AND
   BEAR ME IN YOUR MIND LET ALL THE
   WORLD SAY WHAT THEY WILL SPEEK OF
   ME AS YOU FIND.
A FAVOURIT GIFT
KEEP THIS FOR MY SAKE DARLING
A GIFT FROM ELIZABETH HURST 1859

Curses and Blessings
IF YOU TOUCH IT WILL TAKE
BLESS JACOB
MAY THE PLESOURS OF REST IN OUR
   HARTS
PLENTY AND PLENTY

Family Memorials (birthdays and deaths)
CHARLES BROUNCIL DIED MAY 12 1843
   AGED 22 YEARS AT ASHWOOD IN KENT
   LOST FROM SIGHT BUT STILL IN MIND
JOHN WESTON MY HUSBAND AGED 28
WILLIAM LOVEDAY DEAD AND GON
THOMAS TURNHAM BORN 1760 DIED APRIL
   22 AGED 76
ROSE ADD JUDD DIED JANY 27 1862 AGED 6
   WEEKS
HERWIN HILL HELMDON AGED 22 1844
MARY LANCASTER MY DEAR
   GRANDMOTHER 1871
THOS KIMBLE DIED JULY 6th 1865 AGED 70
   (see figure 37)
FAITH WESLEY BORN MARCH 11 1836
EMILY GWYNN BORN DECEMBER 1 1839

Cryptograms, Puzzles
X UR AND X UB AND XX UR TO ME
   (cross you are and cross you be and
   extra cross you are to me) (see figure 38)
YM EVOL SI TA A ECNATSID TUB ROF
   REVE NO DNIM
   (My love is at a distance but for ever on
   mind)
MAHER SHALAL HASH BAZ WYHES

Religious Subjects
THOSE THAT SEEK SHALL EARLY FIND ME
THE LORD IS MY SHEPHERD
DO NOT STEAL
THOU SHALT NOT STEEL
JESUS DIED FOR ME
JESUS IS LOVE

JESIS DIED FOR ME
REMEMBER JESUS CHRIST
JESUS WEEPT
DEATHS SURE
TIME IS SHORT
   (see figure 38)
REPENT AND BELIEVE THE GOSPEL
JESUS SMIL AND HE LOVE ME TO

Political, Historical, and National Events

MAY THE PRINCE OF WALES BE GLORY
   WED
VICTORIA MARED FEB 10 PRINCE ALBER
   WED FEB 10
   (Pair of bobbins)
QUEEN VICTORIA CROWNED 1838
JUBILEE OF GEORGE III 1810
ALMA 1854
WAR IN EGYPT TEL EL KEBIR 1882
VOTE FOR ALTHORPE
VOTE FOR OSBORNE
CRAWLEY FOR EVER
GUNNING AND REFORM

Famous People

LORD NELSON
JOHN WESLEY
JOHN BUNYAN WAKES OAK
   (Made from oak in Whittlebury forest and supposed to be connected with Hereward the Wake)

Admonitions and Apophthegms

TIME FLIES 1714
NEVER FAINT
MARRY NOT TILL 26
DONT DELAY THE PRESENT DAY
DO GOOD TO ALL
DO NOT BE FORGETFUL
IMPROVE
TIME IS SHORT
TOUCH ME NOT WITHOUT CONSENT
MAID BEFORE YOU MARRY MIND THE
   GOLDEN RUL LOOK BEFORE YOU LEAP
   OR ELSE YOULL PLAY THE FOOL
BETTER DO WELL LATE THAN NEVER
NOTHING VENTURE NOTHING GAIN
DEATHS SHORE
WHEAR TRUE LOVE IS PLANTED IT GROWS

Love and Romance – Declarations of Love

MY DEAR

MY LOVE
MY JOY
MY HART
LOVEY
I LOVE YOU MY DEAR THAT IS TRUE
MY HART IS SO FULL OF LOVE FOR THEE
I LOVE ONLY THEE
MY LOVE SO TRUE AS MINE TO YOU
YOU ARE THE FIRST YOUNG MAN THAT
   EVER WON MY ♥
MY DEAR LOVER
STILL I LOVE U
DANIEL GOODWIN MY LOVE 21
DB I LOVE YOU MY DEAR IT IS TRUE JHHS
JAMES HARPER MY SWEETHEART IS CY
   (shy)
SWEET WILLIAM IS THE LADE I LOVE SO
   TRUE MAY 24 1846
GEORGE BOYCE MARY DEVRICKS SWEET
   HART 1859
TIS LOVE TO YOU MY DEAR I HAVE
JOHN WEBB SUSANNAH READ 1840
MY LOVE FOR THE NO ONE CAN TELL
MY LOVE IS LIKE THE BLOOMING ROSE
SITING ON A STILE MARY HAPPY AS THE
   DAY
MY BOYS IF I AM RAGGED MY HART IS
   TRUE
MY MIND IS FIXED I CANNOT RAINGE I
   LOVE MY CHOICE TOO WELL TO
   CHANGE

Love and Romance – Proposals, Refusals, Acceptance

NAME THE DAY
ELIZABETH WED ME MY LOVE
MARRY ME MY OWN TRUE LOVE
LOVE WILL U MARREY
COME LOVE AND LIVE WITH MY MY DEAR
SWEET ONE BE MINE AND MAKE ME THINE
LET LOVE ABIDE TILL DEATH DIVIDE
LET ME FIX THE WEDDING DAY MY DXAR
THIS RING SO ROUND IS A SHILLING I AM
   READY WHEN YOU ARE WILLING
WHEN WILL YOU FIX THE WEDDING DAY
MY DEAR LOVE ME AND MAKE ME YOUR
   BRIDE
IF YOU ARE READY I AM WILLING TO GIVE
   THE CLAK A SHILLING
IF MY LOVER LOVES IT IS TRUE HE WILL BE
   (see figure 37)
MY DEAR LOVE ME AND LET ME BE YOUR
   WIFE
NAME THE DAY

MARRY BUT DONT TARRY
MARRY ME QUICK AND LOVE ME FOREVER
WILL YOU WED
BUY THE RING
LOVE BUY THE RING
  (see figure 38)
ITS ALL VERY FINE BUT NO LODGE FOR
  YOU MY LAD
JOSEPH IT NO FOR HE KNOW IT
NO LODGE HERE

Love and Romance – Quarrels and Making Up

IT IS HARD TO BE SLITED BY THE ONE YOU
  LOVE
LOVE IS A SHARP THORN
LET NO FALSLOVE GAINE MY HART
RICHARD SLITED BY ONE AS
LET GO
LOVE ME OR LEAVE ME ALONE
MY LOVES BEEN FALSE TO ME AND SHE
  HAS BEEN MY RUIN
I WONCE LOVED THEM THAT NER LOVED
  ME
LET NO FALS LOVE GAINE MY HART
MERCY LOVE (see figure 36)
KEEP YOUR TEMPER
LOVE DONT BE CROSS
  (see figure 38)

Love and Romance – Despair and Absence

MY LOVE IS LOST FOR EVER
ABSENT MAKES THE HART GROE FONDER
LOVE ME AND NO ONE ELSE
I WISH I WAS MARRIED
DONT DECEIVE ME MY LOVE
GONE O MY LOVE
YOUNG MEN ARE DECEITFUL
IF YOU DENY MY LOVE I DY
MY LOVE IS ABSENT
FORGET ME NOT WHEN I ARE AWAY
MY LOVE I LONG TO SE
LOVE DONT TARRY
MY LOVE IS LOST FOREVER
SWEET TIS THE LOVE THAT MEETS
  RETURN BY BITTER WHEN IT MEATS A
  FROWN

Love and Romance – Saucy

DONT TELL MY MOTHER
HUDDLE ME CUDDLE ME
MEET ME BY MOONLIGHT ALONE
THE BOYS LOVE THE GIRLS

KISS ME
KISS ME QUICK MY MOTHER IS COMING
KISS ME QUCK MY MOME IS COMIN
IF I LOVE THE BOYS THAT IS NOTHING TO
  NOBODY
IF I LOVE A LAD IN EAVENSTONE THATS
  NOTHIN TO NOBODY
KISS ME COURT ME HUG ME TITE DONT
  CRUMP MY COIR TONIGHT
  (coir=collar)
DONT KISS AND TELL
I WANTS A HUSBAND
  (see figure 38)

Sailors and Soldiers

DON LIST LOVE
LOVE DONT LIST (enlist)
JACK ALIVE (safe return of a sailor)
JAMES BONNINTON 32 RIDGE M
RICHARD THOMPSON IN HER MAJESTY
  SHIP

Popular Songs and Verses

SLAP BANG HERE WE GO AGAIN
MIX ME DOLLE
O GOD OF JACOB
JESES DIED FOR ME
O JOYFUL WHEN WE MEET TO PART NO
  MOARE
WITH ALL THY FAULTS I LOVE THEE STILL
  (Cowper's *Task*)
WAIT FOR THE WAGGON
POP GOES THE WEASEL
NOT FOR JOSEPH

Miscellaneous

I ONCE HAD A MOTHER LIKE YOU
DONT CRY FOR ME
SUCCESS FOR THE LACE PILLOW
MOTHER WHEN SHALL I MARRY
PEÈP FOOL PEEP PEEP AT YOUR BROTHER
  DID YOU EVER SEE ONE FOOL PEEP AT
  ANOTHER
PEEP FOOL PEEP DINT YOU NEVER SEE A
  BOBIN AFORE
COME UP LITTLE HORSE WILL YOU BUY
  ANY FISH ONE FOR A PENNY TWO FOR A
  KISS
  (Honiton bobbin; see figure 35)

14 Machine-made Lace

To the cottage lace workers of the early eighteenth century the idea of a machine to make lace must have appeared a remote possibility, but by the 1770s the first lace-making machine was already in being. Although the lace-making machines put the hand-made lace workers out of business, for the first time lace was available to the poor as well as to the rich.

It took about 70 years to develop lace-making machinery, from the first machine which produced a type of knitted lace to the very sophisticated machine which produced all types of patterned lace.

During the introduction of this machinery the lace workers struggled on, but by 1830 the machines were so advanced that they outpaced all competition from the hand-workers.

The East Midland lace makers were worst affected because, unlike the Devonshire workers, they could not make use of the new machine-made net. The Honiton workers used the new net and appliquéed their hand-made sprigs on to it. This saved them the laborious work of making the bobbin ground. Unfortunately, Honiton lace made at this time was of a very inferior quality because the sprigs were so badly made. The Midlands workers, whose lace was made all in one piece, tried to compete with the machines by making coarse Torchon and Maltese designs, but the machines worked faster and produced better lace. Eventually machine-made lace was of such high quality that it was hardly

FIGURE 39
Top and bottom:
Pure cotton machine-made lace in ecru;
centre: cotton with silk medallions. All early twentieth century

distinguishable from the hand-made variety.

Today, machine-made lace is so cheap and easily available that lace makers tend to be a little scornful of it. This is unfair, for large amounts of good quality lace can be produced very rapidly, and can be used and enjoyed by a wide variety of buyers.

The first machine-made lace was made on a frame used for making fancy knitted stockings. Modifications to this machine went on for some 40 years, from about 1760 to the end of the eighteenth century. Another eight years elapsed before John Heathcoat produced his transverse warp machine which was capable of imitating the hand-made Lille ground bobbin net. On the Transverse warp machine, the weft threads (those going across the fabric), which normally went in and out of the warp threads (those going down the fabric) were instead twisted around the warp threads, and lain diagonally through the net.

Hammond net

The main centres for the stocking making industry in the eighteenth century were in Nottinghamshire and Leicestershire. Many people worked in stocking factories, but there was also a considerable cottage industry. Workers had stocking frames set up in their own homes, and worked in much the same way as the cottage lace workers. Many home workers in the stocking industry were employed making fancy hosiery and, aware of the fortune awaiting the inventor of a lace machine, probably experimented in their spare time on fancy lace stitches, hoping to invent such a machine.

In 1768, one of these workers, a man called Hammond, managed to do so. Both he and his wife were heavy drinkers and, so the story goes, found themselves in a Nottingham pub one night without any money and, consequently, without a drink. Thoroughly miserable, Hammond sat looking at his wife's cap and caul which were trimmed with broad bobbin lace. Suddenly inspired, he felt sure that he could imitate the lace on his stocking frame. He borrowed some silk, went home,

worked on his frame and, eventually, produced a net which resembled lace. From this net Hammond's wife made caps which sold extremely well. Hammond called this net 'Valenciennes' but it bore no resemblance whatsoever to Valenciennes lace. He went on to make other nets from which purses, mittens and gloves were made and sold. Hammond did not invent bobbin net, for bobbin net was a quite different product. Nevertheless, 'Hammond net' was in demand, sold well, and Hammond made a fair living from the profits.

Point net and other improvements

Others improved on Hammond's method, but the resulting lace was still an openwork knitted, or looped, fabric. One improvement, introduced in 1777, led to a net, known as 'point net', being made. This, however, had nothing to do with the old point lace, but was so called because the lace was made on sharp points. Other improvements on this point net followed and the products were known variously as 'barley-corn', 'square' and 'spider net'.

These were all looped laces, so that if one stitch broke, the whole piece began to unravel. To remedy this, the threads were gummed together, but the lace became stiff and thick. Point net had a hexagonal mesh, and was embroidered by needle-run patterns worked by hand. The mesh was made in great quantities in Nottinghham until about 1809, when it was supplanted by the twisted thread machine-made net invented by John Heathcoat, which was, for the first time, a fairly good imitation of hand-made bobbin net.

The point net industry became quite large, and at its peak employed 15,000 workers in making the net, plus a considerable number of women and girls who were kept busy embroidering the fabric.

The warp frame machine

Another important advance towards a completely machine-made lace was the warp frame machine which was developed from the old stocking frame. This machine also made looped stitches, but it was more successful because instead of using one thread running horizontally, as in ordinary hand knitting, it used several threads which formed chains going down the fabric which were joined together in zig-zag fashion. This stopped the fabric from unravelling if a stitch broke. A type of net called 'Mechlin' was made on this machine, but it bore only a passing resemblance to the real Mechlin ground. This Mechlin net was found to be too elastic and it went out of fashion in 1816. By contrast the 'warp-net' made on this machine still remained in demand for some time after Heathcoat produced his 'twist-net'. In 1830 there was a great demand for 'silk blonde' produced on the warp frame machine, and net with spots was made in 1820.

Heathcoat's twisted net machine

John Heathcoat's twisted net machine was, however, the great break-through in machine made lace as it fulfilled the eighteenth century ambition of reproducing the hand-made bobbin ground by machinery. Since Heathcoat's invention was so important, it is interesting to take a look at the man himself. He was born in Duffield, near Derby, in 1763, the son of Francis and Elizabeth Heathcoat, who were small farmers. John had a brother, Thomas, who eventually became a large manufacturer of bobbin net in Barnstaple, and a sister, Anne Hallam, whose husband later became the director of John's bobbin net factories in Paris and St Quentin.

When John was seven his father went blind and was forced to give up farming. The family moved to Long Whatton, near Loughborough in Leicestershire. John's father supported the family by hiring out warp machinery for making stockings to master stocking makers in the area. John therefore became familiar with machinery from an early age, and when he was old enough he was apprenticed to a Derby ribbed stocking maker and framesmith. At the age of 16 John's overriding ambition was to invent a lace-making machine. To this end he devoted nearly all his spare

time and money, even though he was earning only 25s. (£1.25) a week. He began by watching an old bobbin lace maker at work. He described this experience as follows:

I set to work to inform myself in what peculiarity in the texture of pillow lace consisted and for this purpose obtained a sight of the process of making it. A pretty heap of chaotic material I found it! Like peas in a frying pan dancing about.*

Undaunted, he obtained a piece of bobbin lace which he unravelled. What at first had appeared to be 'an unmanageable and complicated mass of dependent bobbins' finally sorted themselves out into passives and weavers. He then took some pack thread, put up a 'sort of frame', and the lace-making machine was born.

John Heathcoat took out the patent for his bobbin net machine in 1808 when he was only 25 years old. This machine, for the first time ever, made net with twisted sides. The mesh was hexagonal, similar to that of Lille net. This first machine could produce only very narrow widths. The following year John Heathcoat patented another machine which could produce much wider nets. This patent was to run 14 years.

Heathcoat's first machine was affectionately nicknamed 'Old Loughborough'. It gave rise to an enormous lace industry. The net was sometimes used plain but, more often, it was embroidered. This was done either by tambouring (chain stitching) or by needle-run darning. Special blocks were made for printing the pattern on to the net, and some of these have been preserved in the Castle Museum, Nottingham. Picot edgings were made by hand and sewn on to the machine-made lace, for at this stage picots could not be made by machine. This is one way of telling old machine-made lace from hand-made, where the picots were made with the lace in one operation. Another way is by the embroidery, for in needle-run machine-made laces the thread always

* W. A. Felkin, *History of the Machine – Wrought Hosiery and Lace Manufactures*

FIGURE 40
Machine made lace:
Top and bottom:
Cotton guipure in
popular butter
colour; centre: Cotton
and silk needlerun
lace. All early
twentieth century

passes in and out of the holes, while in hand-made lace it goes between the twisted threads. Another difference is that when clothwork was made the hexagonal mesh could still be seen, while in hand-made lace this is not the case, for ground threads are also used to make the clothwork. Limerick lace was made by embroidering the twisted bobbin net, and Carrickmacross was made by the appliqué of very fine muslin on to the net. Sometimes embroidery was added as well.

Heathcoat's lace-making machinery attracted the attentions of the Luddites, bands of working men who raised riots to destroy machinery. They smashed up Heathcoat's factory, destroying 55 of his machines, valued at £10,000, and burning all the lace. The Luddites, if convicted, were originally sentenced to transportation, but in 1812 a new Act was passed which changed the sentence to one of execution. A man called Towle was convicted of the outrage on Heathcoat's factory, and was publicly executed in 1816. Heathcoat sued and was granted £10,000 compensation with the proviso that it should be spent locally. But he never took his compensation.

Heathcoat refused to stay in the Loughborough area where his life had been endangered. 'I will' he said, 'go as far off as possible from such desperate men as these frame breakers are.' Salvaging what he could of his equipment, and taking a small band of his workers with him, he moved to Tiverton in Devon and set up in business there. The Lille type of net which Heathcoat produced had the typical two twists, but he also made another net with three twists, which had a diamond rather than a hexagonal mesh. It was a lighter more airy fabric, and was known as 'Brussels net'. This three-twist net was in very great demand by the Honiton lace makers who found it an ideal background for their sprigs.

Heathcoat's factory is still in operation today. It produces net on the original Heathcoat machines, although the net is mostly made of nylon instead of silk and cotton. Most of the nylon net is sold as a base to embroidery manufacturers. A small quantity of bridal silk veiling is also produced. Although the factory was taken over in 1969 by the Coats Patons Group, the Heathcoat-Amory family still retain a financial interest.

The pusher

The next important development was a pusher, a machine capable of putting pattern into the twist net. Although it could produce clothwork, it could not put in the outlining gimp threads. This latter process was carried out by hand. Nevertheless, the pusher came the closest to imitating hand-made bobbin lace. A later version of the pusher made the East Midlands honeycomb ground, known as 'Grecian net'. In the 1870s the pusher also made a very good imitation black silk Chantilly. Sometimes only hand-run gimp could distinguish this Chantilly from the real thing. It was very popular in the 1860s for making parasols, the black lace being mounted on white silk, a combination of which was then very fashionable. Black Chantilly was also used for the very large shawls which hung down over crinoline skirts, and also for veils and capes.

Later developments

John Leavers was responsible for patterned lace made entirely by machine. He gave his name to the well-known patterned lace still made, often by Leavers machines, in Nottingham today. In 1809 Leavers made a machine similar in principle to Heathcoat's net machine. Modifications to the Leavers machines using the system invented by Joseph Marie Jacquard in 1805 resulted in the manufacture of lace, with or without a net ground, entirely by machine. The last and most difficult operation, of incorporating the

thick gimp outlining thread into machine-made lace was overcome in 1841.

By 1860 there were so many lace manufacturers in the country that the market was flooded with lace. A square yard of lace which would have cost £5 in 1810 cost only 6d. (2½p) in 1860. Fortunately for the British lace industry, there was a great demand for English machine-made net in France. English machines were far superior to those of the French and turned out a much better product. France's lace manufacturers were anxious to acquire an English machine, but export of these was strictly prohibited. In spite of this, one was secretly smuggled into France in 1816. Subsequent technical developments in English lace-making machines, however, continued to give the British manufacturers the edge over their French rivals. Nottingham became, and still remains, the centre of English lace making.

FIGURE 41
Machine-made insertions in ecru colour. Cotton net with silk embroidery. Late nineteenth century

15 Other Laces

Tatting and knotting

Tatting requires only very simple equipment: one or two special shuttles around which the thread is wound, and a small hook. The work is composed of only three basic stitches, a single stitch, a double stitch and a picot. The stitches are worked over a running thread and either pulled up into rings or loops or left as chain bars. The single stitch resembles a buttonhole stitch and the double stitch is just a continuation of the single stitch. The picot, or purl, is made by leaving a loop of thread between the double stitches. The most difficult part when learning is to hold the thread properly, but this is soon mastered with the aid of a good teacher.

In the early days of tatting, the rings and loops were made separately but later a technique using netting needles made it possible to join the rings together while

FIGURE 42
Simple tatted motifs
made by the author

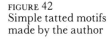

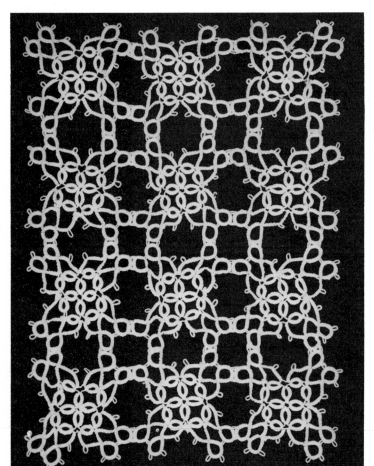

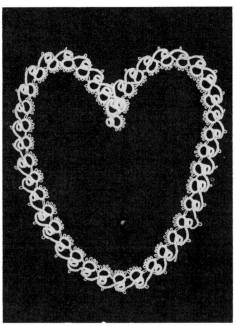

FIGURE 43
Tatted edging made
by the author

working the pattern. The netting needles were eventually dispensed with, and a small metal hook used instead. Sometimes this was attached to a small ring which was slipped over the thumb. It was then ready to be picked up quickly. Most modern tatters prefer a separate hook. A further development was the use of two shuttles or a ball of thread and a shuttle. Originally, tatted lace and trimmings were made in white lace thread, but now almost any coloured thread is used.

The art of tatting is believed to have originated in Italy in the sixteenth century, but it was not widely practised in Britain until the nineteenth century. It seems to have developed naturally from the art of knotting, which was introduced into Britain towards the end of the seventeenth century and continued in popularity for the next hundred years. Tatting then took its place. Both tatting and knotting involve a similar technique using a shuttle and thread, but while tatting produces a dainty lace fabric or trimming in its entirety (see figure 44), knotting produces a decorative thread or cord resembling a string of beads, which is couched on to fabric as a surface embroidery or fringe. A form of knotting which produced extra large knots or picots had the mouth-watering name of 'sugar plum'.

Once knotting and tatting have been mastered, they are so simple to do that they require little concentration, and the work proceeds by touch rather than sight. They were very useful occupations in the candle-lit evenings of the eighteenth and nineteenth centuries, when the light was too poor for fine needlework.

Knotting was considered a ladylike and elegant occupation, and in the eighteenth

FIGURE 44
Evening bag with tatted decoration worked in fine No. 60 cotton. Made by the author

century ladies loved to have their portraits painted showing them with large ornate knotting shuttles in their hands. There are several such famous portraits, e.g. by Reynolds and Nattier.

Knotting was also popular at court. Ladies, often required to wait for many hours in order to see a member of the royal family, passed the time in knotting. It was also a suitable occupation for long, bumpy journeys in the badly sprung coaches of the seventeenth and eighteenth centuries. Mary, William III's wife, was an ardent knotter, although she was ridiculed by Sir Charles Sedley, for what was then regarded as a homely occupation:

> For here's a Queen, no thanks to God!
> When rides in coach abroad
> Is always knotting thread.

The French referred to knotting as '*la frivolité*', the name by which tatting is known in France today. The Italians still call it '*occhi*', which means eyes, because of the rings or 'eyes' from which the designs are made up. The English name, 'tatting', is supposed to be derived from the French word 'tater', to touch, but another theory is that it comes from the word 'tatty' because in the beginning the rings and loops were made in pieces and joined together afterwards by tying or sewing.

Old knotting and tatting shuttles were made of many different materials, including ivory, tortoiseshell, mother-of-pearl, wrought steel, silver, gold, amber, porcelain, horn and painted wood. Many were elaborately decorated. The tatting shuttle is smaller than the knotting shuttle, which was over 150cm (6in.) long and 2½cm (1in.) wide. The ends of the latter were also wider apart to take the thick homespun yarn often used. Another difference is that tatting shuttles have rather more pointed ends. French knotting shuttles were particularly ornate and larger than the English ones.

Macramé

Macramé is derived from an Arabic word which means 'ornamental fringe'. Macramé has evolved from the arts of netting and knotting. It is one of the oldest types of lace known. The Spanish and Italians made it in the sixteenth century, the latter calling it '*punto a groppo*'. It was made commercially along the Italian Riviera in the nineteenth century to decorate the fringes of towels, and was one way of providing employment for people thrown out of work by the introduction of machine-made lace.

It is easy to make, being based on sailors' knots. Sailors called it 'square netting' or 'McNamara's Lace'. Only two basic knots are required: a half hitch (clove hitch), and a flat knot (reef knot). It is the way in which the knots are used which forms the pattern.

Macramé work came to Britain at about the end of the seventeenth century, in the reign of William and Mary. It was a very popular pastime in the Victorian era. Macramé was made in large quantities for fringing shawls and for trimming antimacassars, mantel-piece cloths, lamp shades and table covers.

There is a current revival of macramé work, most of which can hardly be classed as lace. It is mainly coarse work for plant holders, wall hangings, bags and belts.

Tambour work and net laces

Tambour work was originally a surface embroidery of chain stitch. It became classed as a lace when it was worked on machine-made net. It was referred to as 'tambour work' because the material to be worked was stretched tightly between two rings or hoops resembling a drum or tambour. The old tambour hoops were made of wood or iron, one hoop being slightly smaller than the other and lined with cork or velvet, or bound with ribbon to prevent the material from sagging. Many hoops were fixed onto wooden stands, so that both hands of the embroiderer could move freely above and below the work. It is possible to do tambour work with modern embroidery hoops, working the chain stitch with a needle. The work proceeds slowly, but the result is much the same.

A tambour hook was made of metal, and was similar to a crochet hook, except that the point was smaller and less curved, and was fixed into a wooden handle for a better grip. The hook was held vertically above the fabric to be embroidered, and pushed through it, catching up the thread which was held beneath the left hand. A small loop was then pulled up and through the fabric to the front of it. A second loop was pulled through, and the first loop slipped over it, exactly as one would work a crochet chain. The stitches were worked very evenly and spaced about 2mm (1/10in.) apart. Fine thread was used for muslin and net, but coloured silks, chenille, woollen and metal threads were used on heavier materials. There were no set rules however, and the ladies of bygone centuries loved to experiment with their designs and materials.

Tambour work needed a long unbroken thread which flowed freely and evenly, and many types of holders were devised. Some were box-like frames while others were reels fitted beneath the tambour frame stand. Since tambouring was an occupation for ladies of fashion they had to have thread holders which were in keeping with their style of dress, so they wore elegant, richly ornamented tambouring reel holders attached to their waist belts by equally ornamental clasps.

Tambour work was of Eastern origin, and was known for many centuries in China, Persia, India and Turkey before it was introduced into France and subsequently into Britain. It was well established in Britain by the mid-eighteenth century, and was produced on a commercial scale by 1780, particularly in the Scottish districts of Lanarkshire and Renfrewshire where thousands of young girls and women were employed in 'flowering' muslin with tambour work. The designs were usually floral sprigs and trails. Sprigged muslin became very popular for the high-waisted dresses with deep embroidered hems that were worn at the end of the eighteenth century. One of these fashionable tamboured muslin dresses cost about 18s. (90p) in 1807. Tambour lace was the result of the invention of machine-made bobbin net. The first machines could not embroider net, and this was done by hand, either by tambouring or darning with a needle.

Tambour lace was made in Coggeshall,

Essex, from about 1812, and also in North America, but it did not reach Ireland for another 17 years. Although it is usually said that tambour lace went to Ireland via Nottingham, the people of Coggeshall claim that Charles Walker, a nineteenth-century resident of Coggeshall, spent a holiday in Ireland, returning there in 1829 with 24 Coggeshall workers. He settled near Limerick, and set up schools to train young girls in the art of tambouring and darning net. Henceforth the lace became known as Limerick lace, an example of which is shown in figure 45. The Limerick industry was short-lived, for Walker sold his factory to a bankrupt and was never paid for it. He died in poverty in 1842. The

FIGURE 45
Limerick lace;
nineteenth century

Coggeshall workers either returned to Essex or emigrated to America. It is doubtful whether the industry would have survived anyway, for in 1841 machine-embroidered bobbin net was introduced. Limerick lace reached a very high standard during the 1830s. Of the two types of lace, the needle-run variety was by far the most delicate, but it was also more costly.

Coggeshall lace was only tamboured, although occasionally darning was added. The Coggeshall lace industry is now being revived and is producing some very beautiful, if costly works of art.

Carrickmacross was another lace based on machine-made net. It is so called because two sisters named Reid started a small school near Carrickmacross in Ireland to teach the local peasant women to make the lace. During the 1840s potato famine in Ireland the industry was enlarged to provide work for local people who would otherwise have starved. Fine muslin was appliquéed on to the net, usually surrounded by a cordonnet. Occasionally the net was cut to make open-work fillings, and sometimes darning was used as well. Guipure Carrickmacross had no net backing. The muslin motifs surrounded by the cordonnet were joined together by bars. It is not a very strong lace, does not stand up to washing and is difficult to iron.

Filet lace

This is also known as 'lacis' or darned netting. The net was usually square meshed and hand-knotted, although occasionally diamond-shaped mesh was used. The Spanish in particular used a diamond mesh. The netting was usually made with a shuttle and mesh sticks, in the same way as fishing nets are produced.

The net was darned in and out of the mesh, and different thicknesses of thread

FIGURE 46
Carrickmacross lace vine pattern; nineteenth century

were used to produce a textured pattern.
The patterns were darned in blocks. This
is a very old technique dating back to
the ancient Egyptian era, and there are
still some twelfth-century specimens in
museums.

Filet lace was very popular in Victorian
times, and was made into curtains, side-
board runners, chair back and bedcovers,
but it was seldom, if ever, used for
clothing.

Knitted lace

Knitting is so familiar that it hardly needs
describing. It is one of the oldest known
crafts and can be traced back to the time of
Christ, where it was well established as a
domestic craft in the Middle East. The
technique of working was different, since
the very early knitting needles were
hooked at the end like modern crochet
hooks, the thread being held in the left
hand.

Knitted lace was never a 'grand' lace,
nor was it made on a commercial scale.
Knitted lace was made in homes for hundreds of years. There is a beautiful
example of old knitted lace in the Christ-
church Museum of Ipswich in Suffolk; it is
a baby's bonnet which dates from the
second quarter of the seventeenth century.

During the second half of the eighteenth century, and the first part of the
nineteenth century, knitted lace became
extremely fashionable. Semi-transparent
muslins were being imported from India in
ever increasing quantities towards the end
of the eighteenth century for fashionable
wear in England. This created a demand
for dainty white accessories. Since there
was a heavy import tax on all foreign-
produced laces, finest white cotton was
knitted into lace to make gloves, mittens,
collars, cuffs, fichus, bonnets and reti-
cules, doyleys and table centres.

The work was so intricate and the
thread so fine that finest gauge steel
needles were necessary, many of them
being little thicker than ordinary sewing
needles. It was often difficult to see the fine
white cotton on the silver-steel needles so a
technique of 'blueing' the centre of the
needles was used to help show up the

FIGURE 47
Irish crochet dress
circa 1902 made in
Youghal Co. Cork.

Reproduced by
permission of
National Museum of
Ireland, Dublin

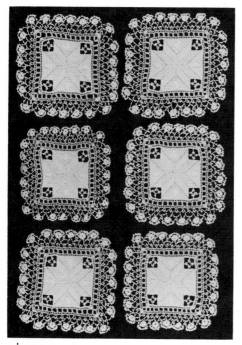

FIGURE 48
Set of fine crochet
table mats, late
nineteenth century

FIGURE 49
Detail of mat showing
raised flowers, late
nineteenth century

stitches.

The vogue for fine white knitting faded out in the late 1820s.

Crochet

Crochet and tambour work employ similar techniques, but whereas tambour lace is surface embroidery on net, crochet lace is complete in itself. For this reason the French gave it the name of 'crochet in the air'. The name crochet is derived from the French words 'crochet' or 'croc' meaning 'hook'. It was sometimes called 'poor man's lace'.

Irish crochet was probably the most perfect and beautiful of all hand-made crochet lace. It differed from ordinary crochet in that padding was used in many of the designs to make certain motifs stand out in bold relief in a way that resembled Venetian raised point needle laces. Although the designs for Irish crochet were very elaborate, they were in fact reasonably easy to work once the technique had been

mastered. The method of working differed from that of ordinary crochet because the motifs were worked separately and later joined together with a dainty background called 'filling', in much the same way as with Honiton lace.

The motifs usually found in Irish crochet lace were shamrocks, leaf sprays, roses, wheels, daisies, bells and bunches of grapes. The filling stitches included single picot loop, double picot loop, clones knot and open space fillings, the last being considered the most dainty of all. Several thicknesses of thread were used as padding to give the raised effect. Padded rings, as used in the bunch of grapes motif, were made by winding the thread a number of times round the finger or pencil, and working over it with double or treble crochet. Another method was to buttonhole over the rings with needle and thread using, in fact, needlepoint techniques.

The design for the lace was traced on to linen. The motifs were then worked and tacked into place on the pattern, and the

filling was then worked round them.

Like tatting, crochet was known in Italy and the bordering countries in the sixteenth century where it was called 'nun's lace' for it was worked almost exclusively by nuns in the religious houses. The technique of crochet was also well established in Spain by the end of the eighteenth century, but it did not become widely popular in Britain until the early nineteenth century.

In the British Isles, the Irish were first to take up crochet, and by the mid-nineteenth century an industry had already been established in several areas of Ireland. The work was widely taught in convent schools to the children of the poor. The main centres of the Irish industry were Monaghan and Clones in the north and Cork in the south. The Irish crochet industry also helped to ward off starvation during the famine years.

Fine crochet was introduced into England in 1820 by Eleanore Riego de la Branchardière. The daughter of a French nobleman who fled to England during the French Revolution, she devoted all her time to developing the art of crochet in her adopted country. She worked out many complicated patterns and for two years, from 1852 until 1854, produced *The Needle*, a monthly journal in which she published patterns. Some of these fine crochet patterns remained in use for over 100 years. For this work very fine metal hooks were always used. Crochet hooks of bone, tortoiseshell, ivory and wood were used only for wool or thick thread.

Ayrshire work

Ayrshire work, also called 'Scotch hole', was not truly a lace but a combination of fine white embroidery and needlepoint lace filling stitches. The work was very delicate and beautiful. It was composed of graceful flower designs and sprays worked on very fine muslin or linen. The designs are outlined in fine satin stitch with needlepoint lace filling stitches, tiny eyelet

FIGURE 50
Crochet resembling
filet lace worked in
trebles by Violet
Spong circa 1920

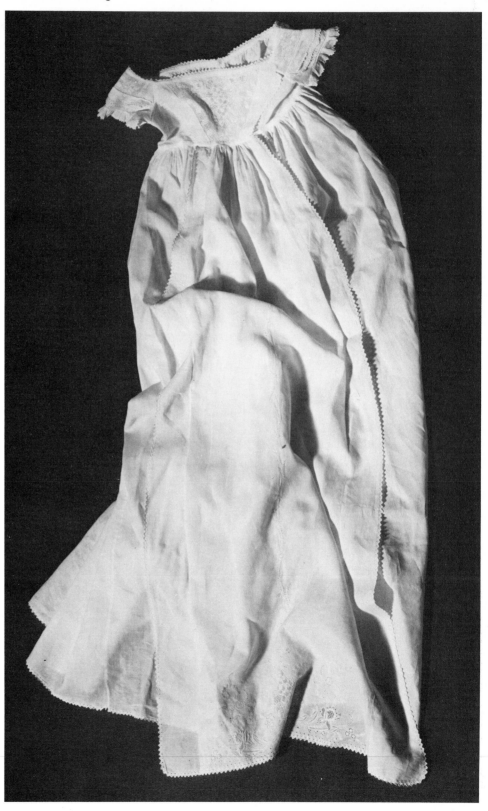

FIGURE 51A
Ayrshire gown in fine
lawn; mid-nineteenth
century

FIGURE 51B
Ayrshire gown; detail

FIGURE 52
Detail of Ayrshire
gown showing
embroidery on
bottom edge which
matches bodice

holes, stem stitch and beading stitches. The charm of the work lay in the contrast and variety of needlepoint stitches. The fillings were worked on a base of drawn threadwork, and not on a skeleton of threads laid down first.

Ayrshire work was used for perelines (wide fichu-like collars), cuffs, flounces, frilly caps, muslin collars and tippets, but the most exquisite work was to be found on infants' gowns, caps, bonnets and christening robes. A characteristic feature of these gowns was a triangle of embroidery in the front of the long skirt bordered by separate wings or flounces. The bodice had an inverted triangle decorated with the same design as the skirt on a smaller scale. Sometimes the point of the triangle on the bodice was carried down over the skirt and left detached. The gowns had square necklines, back openings and tiny puffed sleeves. The older gowns had several frills over the shoulders. An Ayrshire gown was presented to Queen Victoria in 1841 for the infant Prince of Wales.

Ayrshire work gowns were made of fine muslin, but the caps and bonnets were made of fine, sheer linen cambric. It was possible to buy not only complete robes and caps, but also parts of garments such as bodices, cap crowns and bonnet circles; thus one may come across a cap or gown where the design on one part is quite different from that on another.

The wide range of garments available in Ayrshire work is shown in this advertisement in the *Edinburgh Evening Courant* in September 1843:

> . . . Six hundred lace perelines from 1/9 to 3/6 . . . immense stock of muslin perelines, chemisettes, morning caps and cuffs. Collars . . . comprising every style and shape from the plainest to the finest specimens of Ayrshire needlework. A wonderfully large stock of Infants' long ROBES. . . . French cambric caps, frock bodices, crowns etc. flouncing edging and trimmings. . . .

This charming white work was first introduced into Ayrshire around 1820 by Mrs Jamieson, an agent for the existing tambour work cottage industry. She had

seen a baby's robe embroidered with fine needlepoint lace stitches which had been brought to Scotland from Sicily. The work had been done by a French woman.

Ayrshire work was always known locally as 'sewn muslin', which was its trade name, or 'floorerin' (flowering) by the workers. It later became known as 'Scotch hole work', or simply as 'Scotch hole'. The work was highly fashionable in the mid-nineteenth century, and was exported in large quantities to Europe, Russia, Germany, Dublin and London. From Ayrshire the 'sewn muslin' skills extended to Lanarkshire and Renfewshire and even as far afield as Madeira, where the work was introduced when the grape harvest failed disastrously. The workers in Madeira had to use blue thread instead of the traditional white because the hot climate made their hands perspire and soiled the white thread. The craft spread from Scotland to Ireland in 1830, and the Irish girls mastered the skills so rapidly that they were soon exporting their work back to Glasgow to be sold as 'Ayrshire work'.

During the 1830s and 1840s thousands of young Irish and Scottish girls were employed on Ayrshire work. The youngsters often worked in workrooms together, while the older women worked at home in much the same way as did the old bobbin-lace makers. The women earned 1s. (5p) a day. It must have required a continuous concentrated effort to earn this amount for the workers did not even stop to thread needles. They paid a child 1d. (a little under ½p) a week for this chore. In the workrooms several girls often worked on one single piece of embroidery, each using her own particular skill in much the same way as the Brussels lace workers. The women at home often clustered together in one cottage to share candlelight and fires.

The designs were transferred to the muslin by large wooden stamps or by a carved roller rubbed over the old fashioned blue-bag. If the worker wanted a design for herself she would sometimes spread a piece of muslin over a worked design and rub with the back of a pewter spoon.

By the mid-nineteenth century the industry was simultaneously at its peak of prosperity and on the edge of decline. The imminent decline was due to three factors: the American Civil War, which drastically curtailed the export of American cotton to Scotland; the change of fashion from the crinoline with its full flounces and trimmings to the bustle which required heavier, richer fabrics; and lastly, but most damaging of all, the invention of embroidery machinery. The Swiss had invented, and put into commercial use as early as 1840, a machine which copied Ayrshire embroidery. The Swiss poached the Scottish export trade to America by shipping their goods via Hamburg. As a result the Americans called the Swiss embroidery 'Hamburgs'. By 1870 the Scottish and Irish Ayrshire work industries were virtually dead.

FIGURE 53
Teneriffe lace

FIGURE 54
Lace tablets for
Teneriffe lace.
Reproduced by
permission of Castle
Museum, York

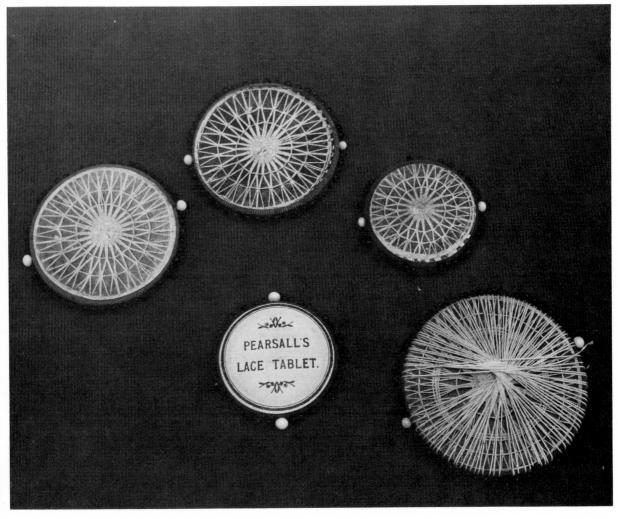

FIGURE 55
'Five o'clock' cloth
with cutwork and
drawn work; late
nineteenth century

Teneriffe lace

Another name for this was 'sun lace'. The name was derived from needlework called *'sols'* which was made in Spain in the sixteenth century. In the original form, circles were cut in material, radiating threads were placed across the holes and embroidered upon. The work spread from Spain to Southern and Central America and from there to the Canary Islands.

The work gradually developed until circular pieces of lace were made without fabric. Circles were drawn on parchment and outlined with running stitches. The radiants were then taken through opposite pairs of running stitches and embroidered as before.

Eventually the whole process was simplified even further by the use of a lace tablet – two circles of cardboard glued together with pins all round the edge. This made work much easier since the thread could be wound round the pins straight from the spool.

Teneriffe work was very popular in Britain in the Victorian era, but little was made after the turn of the century. Perhaps now that so many British tourists are visiting the Canary Islands the art of making this attractive lace may be revived in Britain.

16 Lace Making Today

There has been a remarkable revival of interest in lace making of all kinds during the past decade. In sharp contrast to the lace makers of bygone centuries, to whom a yard or two of lace meant the difference between a full or empty stomach, we can make lace for pleasure. Many people have grown tired of ready-made entertainment, and are turning for relaxation to the old, half-forgotten crafts, and are finding pleasure and satisfaction in using their creative talents.

Lace making is a versatile occupation. One can work in companionable groups or alone. Although it is easier to learn to make bobbin lace with the help of a teacher, it is possible to teach oneself, and once the basics have been learnt one can experiment with old and new designs, different types of lace, threads, textures and colour, the only real limit being one's own imagination.

In the 1960s few people had heard of bobbin lace, and fewer still could make it. Now lace-making classes are held regularly all over Britain and in many other parts of the world. Most classes have been started in response to public demand, but as more and more people are becoming proficient in the craft they are teaching others, and the art of lace making is spreading rapidly.

FIGURE 56
Norwich Lace School which has three generations from one family as students

A typical lace school began like this in Norwich. It was started in 1974 by Patricia Payne who was asked by a friend to teach her Torchon lace making. The news spread and Pat Payne soon found herself with a class of 13 ambitious students in her own home. The local education authority eventually agreed to make the classes official, and on the first enrolment night there were sufficient students for three classes. One of the Norwich classes is shown in figure 56, and this particular class is unique for in it are three generations of lace makers, daughter, mother and grandmother, such is the fascination of lace. The Norwich school has now formed itself into the Norfolk Lace Makers' Association.

Lace makers all over the world are forming themselves into similar associations and classes, and meeting together regularly to exchange patterns and ideas, and to draw inspiration from each other's work.

In Britain, a Lace Guild was formed in 1976, and the membership has now reached well over 1,700, with members scattered all over the globe. The guild keeps lace makers in touch with each other and with other associations and groups. It publishes a quarterly magazine, *Lace*, which is mailed to every member. This reports on various lace-making events taking place both in Britain and abroad. It advertises classes, courses, lace days, and keeps members up to date on suppliers of equipment and threads.

A similar guild was formed in Australia in 1979 with an initial 119 members. Membership has now reached 271, and is still growing. This is a marvellous achievement considering the vast distances to be covered in Australia. Nevertheless, enthusiasts happily travel hundreds of miles from the outback to attend lace classes or lace days. The Lace Guild of Australia is currently working on a plan to have a travelling exhibition to tour the various states and country centres in order to reach older members and those who cannot travel. Many of the Australian teachers are British emigrants who still retain close links with Britain.

The people of New Zealand have been no less enterprising. A lace-makers association was formed in Auckland in 1970 by a determined lady called Alwynne Crowsen who successfully disproved the theory that one cannot learn to make lace from a book. Now the association has 100 members. The New Zealand Lace Making Association is a member of the British Guild.

Canada has a long established lace group, the Denman Island Lacemakers, which was formed in 1919. They meet regularly and hold lace days. In 1979 they held a very special lace day to celebrate their sixtieth anniversary. From this group other lace making groups formed on the mainland of Vancouver, British Columbia, and in 1980 the Vancouver Lace Club held a special lace luncheon to celebrate their twenty-fifth anniversary (1955 to 1980). For this occasion some very special commemorative hand-painted bobbins were made. They were decorated with the floral emblem of British Columbia, the dogwood. Some delightful little lace-making dolls were also hand made by members as souvenirs. Lace making has now spread to many other parts of Canada. The Canadian lace-makers do not have a guild of their own but become members of the International Old Lacers of the USA. In its own words the International Old Lacers is for 'people who love lace . . . who like to study, to make, to collect and to use lace.'

The International Old Lacers organization was originally started in 1953 by four ladies who became interested in the lace on dolls bought for their doll collections. Other lace makers and collectors joined the organization until, in 1979, the membership numbered over 1,250, of which about 275 members come from countries outside America.

On the Continent, lace is being revived as a hobby. In Belgium there is one state-subsidised school in Bruges which teaches lace making, but to achieve the coveted status of Maître Dentellier (Master Lace Maker) at least six years' study and practice are necessary.

Hand-made lace demands so much time and skill that it is not a commercial proposition any longer. Tourists who visit Belgium demand souvenirs of hand-made lace at machine-made prices. To meet the

FIGURE 57
'Lady and gentleman'
pictures made by Mrs
G. Waters, Norwich
Lace School

FIGURE 58 *far left*
Three marine life
pictures made by Mrs
L. Thomas, Norwich
Lace School. Starfish
and Jellyfish were
designed by her

FIGURE 59 *left*
Design taken from a
Hungarian stamp
made by Mrs M.
Herron, Norwich
Lace School

FIGURE 60
Top: mat of modern
lace design by Mrs E.
Yeates, Norwich Lace
School; bottom:
Torchon lace baby's
jacket made by Pat
Payne, teacher,
Norwich Lace School

FIGURE 62
Buckinghamshire lace
mat made by Mrs J.
Symonds

FIGURE 63
Modern Swedish lace
made by Mrs I.
Andrew, Norwich
Lace School

FIGURE 63A
Modern Greek lace
'Bebilla'

FIGURE 64
Modern bobbins
made by Paul Durst

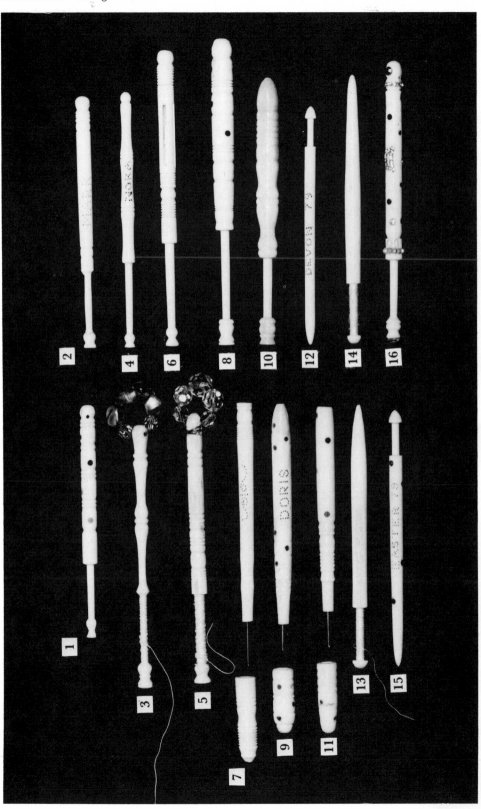

demand, lace is sold to tourists as typical Brussels lace, but it is in fact a machine-made tape formed into circles and sewn together by hand. Another lace sold as 'Belgium' lace is made in Hong Kong and China. Old traditional patterns are sent to the Far East where lace is made by cheap labour using inferior thread; it is then shipped back to Belgium and sold. Most tourists fail to notice the difference.

There are still a few genuine lace makers left in Belgium, but they are nearly all over 70, and as one of them commented, 'You have to be hungry to do this work today.' The dedicated hobbyists, though, tour the country in order to learn how to make the genuine old laces, such as Rose Point, Duchesse or Binche.

The trend in modern lace making is away from lace trimmings and edgings by the yard, and towards more decorative and creative art forms such as lace pictures and wall decorations. The delightful picture of the 'Lady and Gentleman' (figure 57), and three 'Marine Animals' (figure 58) and the charming peacock design mat, cleverly copied from a Hungarian postage stamp (figure 59), are all examples of modern flare and creativity. All these pieces of work were made at the Norwich Lace School, as was the beautiful little baby jacket in Torchon pattern (see figure 60, bottom). Another piece of experimental lace is the brown silk mat made on a 'daisy winder' linked with crochet. This is not bobbin lace, of course. Other examples of modern lace are shown in figures 62, 63 and 63A.

Ten years ago any aspiring lace maker was faced with the daunting prospect of making all her own equipment before she could even begin to learn to make the lace. There were only a few specialist suppliers who stocked a limited range of goods. Pillows presented no problems because they were relatively simple to make, and today many lace makers still prefer to make their own, but to make bobbins in any number provided quite a challenge to one's ingenuity. One had to be very determined and enthusiastic to become a lace maker. Now there are plenty of suppliers who stock everything from pillows to pins. Some suppliers are now stocking poly-

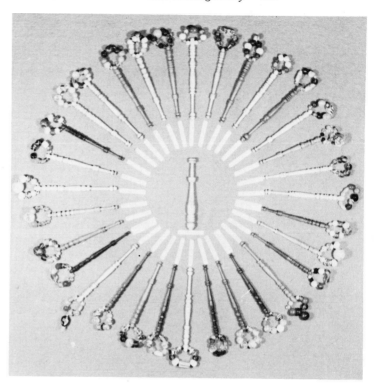

FIGURE 65
Collection of modern wooden bobbins to show colour of different woods. Made by Colin Payne

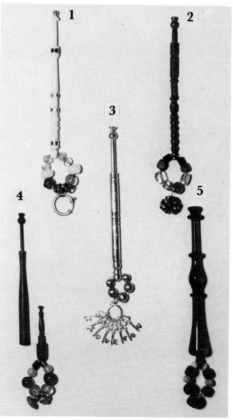

FIGURE 66
Selection of modern bobbins: (1) Bone set with gold and diamond in top; (2) Copper mother-in-babe; (3) Silver made by Colin Payne for his silver wedding anniversary. The keys spell 'I LOVE YOU'; (4) Cow-in-calf; (5) Blue glass

styrene pillows, which have the advantage of being light-weight. Even prickings can be bought, an unheard of luxury in the 1960s.

One of the most exciting developments is the number of craftsmen who have become interested in producing lace-making equipment in traditional styles. Some of the bone and wooden bobbins designed by these modern craftsmen will certainly be collectors' pieces in the future. Many of them are replicas of eighteenth and nineteenth century bobbins, and are as carefully turned, decorated and in-scribed as the antique ones. An example of this beautiful craftsmanship is the set of bone bobbin and hooks made by Paul Durst and shown in figure 64. Also very interesting is the collection of superb wooden bobbins shown in figure 65. Each

of the 33 bobbins has been made from a different type of wood. Figure 66(3) shows a unique modern bobbin made for a silver wedding anniversary. The small keys at the bottom spell out 'I love you'. In the same photograph there is a glass bobbin (see figure 66(5)), and a bone one set with a diamond in gold on the top (see figure 66(1)).

Also by Paul Durst is the bobbin winder shown in figure 67. It is an authentic re-production of an antique design, but has two modern improvements: an automatic reel-feed which eliminates the hand winding of the thread on the yarningales, and a spring clip bobbin holder which stops bobbin wobble and takes any size of bobbin.

For the lace maker on a small budget, plastic bobbins can be bought relatively

FIGURE 67
Bobbin winder by Paul Durst. Note the automatic reel feed and the spring clip bobbin holder

cheaply. They are not as pleasant to use or as attractive to look at as the antique wooden and bone ones, and they do tend to become sticky if one's hands get hot, but they are useful for beginners and children. Even cheaper are home-made bobbins, e.g. from wooden dowelling cut into suitable lengths and shaped with a knife and sand paper. They are not so elegant, but they work. Those shown in figure 68 have been in use for over 20 years.

Other types of lace need far less equipment to make than bobbin lace, but they do need special equipment. Tambour hooks and net for Limerick and Coggeshall lace, not previously available, can now be obtained from suppliers. In fact, all lace makers are catered for by today's suppliers. Figure 69 shows a table centre in heavy écru thread in modern Italian design.

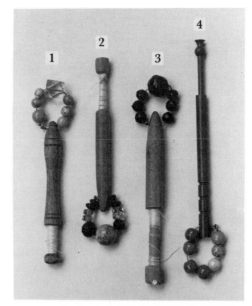

FIGURE 68
Cheap modern bobbins: (1) Modern turned wood; (2) and (3) Hand whittled from dowelling; (4) Cheap modern plastic

FIGURE 69
Table centre in heavy ecru thread, modern Italian design, made by the author

17 Recognising Lace

BOBBIN LACE

To the unskilled eye bobbin lace looks very complicated to make because of the large number of bobbins involved. A simple edging requires about 30 pairs, while a wide flounce may require 500 pairs, but the lace maker only manipulates four bobbins (two pairs) at a time, and all the stitches are built up from only two basic movements, crossing and twisting.

In order to make a cross the required number of bobbins are hung in position on the pillow, and the worker selects four bobbins (two pairs). She then lifts the two centre bobbins and lays the left-hand bobbin over the right-hand bobbin, as shown in diagram 27a.

To make a twist she selects the second and fourth bobbins from the left and moves them to the left, laying them over the first and third bobbins, as shown in diagram 27b. She has now completed a *half stitch*.

To make a whole stitch she works another cross stitch as before. (See diagram 27c.) The sequence of a whole stitch is cross, twist, cross.

A succession of whole stitches worked across the pillow, through a number of pairs of bobbins, produces a piece of cloth-work, which looks exactly the same as plain weaving. A succession of half stitches worked with the same four bobbins produces a plait or braid (as shown in diagram 28 and figure 70). Small loops, called picots, can be added to either or both sides of a plait.

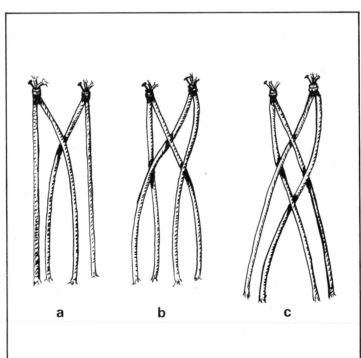

Diagram 27
Basic movements in bobbin lace:
(a) cross; (b) cross and twist (half stitch); (c) cross, twist, cross (whole stitch)

a   b   c

Diagram 28
Plait formed by repeated half stitches

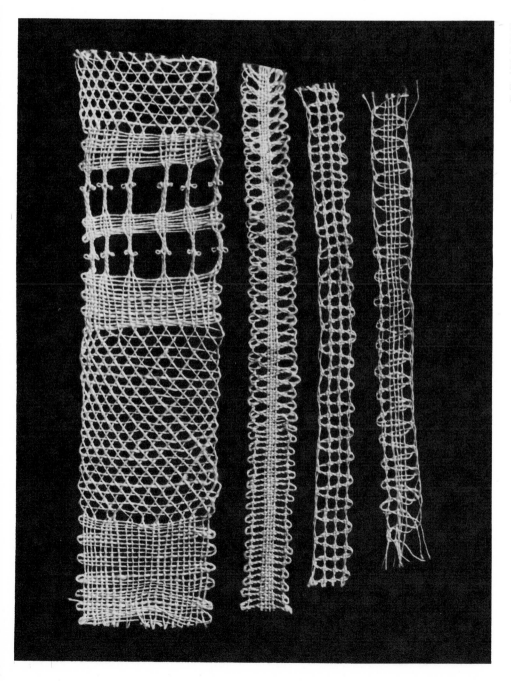

FIGURE 70
Sample strip: half
stitch; whole stitch;
plaits with picots;
various braids and
footings with twisted
and straight passives

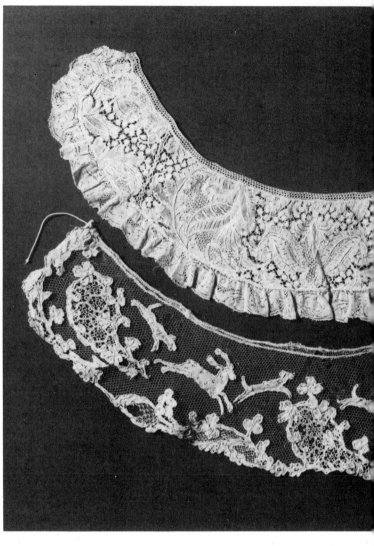

FIGURE 72
Top: Binche collar;
bottom: Alençon
collar, Reproduced
by permission of
Norfolk Museums
Service, Norwich

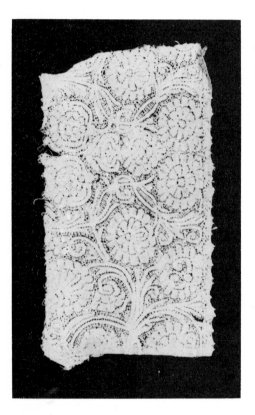

FIGURE 71
Flemish lace circa
1660. See identical
pattern on right hand
side

The half stitch, whole stitch and plait are the three fundamental stitches in bobbin lace. By varying the two basic crossings and twisting movements, more than 250 different stitches can be made.

The worker should always watch the threads in her lace, never the bobbins. This was called by the old lace makers 'learning the lace'. In this way a practised eye can see instantly if a thread has been misplaced and correct it before the lace has proceeded too far.

The following are descriptions of the main types of bobbin lace. From time to time, one comes across regional variations, but it is not difficult to classify the lace into one of the main categories.

Belgium

Many laces which are classified as 'Belgium' laces are Flemish or Dutch, for Belgium did not exist as a country until 1833. Strictly speaking Belgium laces are only those of the nineteenth century. For the sake of convenience, laces which are generally considered to be Belgian today are grouped here.

Flemish (Dutch): Seventeenth Century

This lace is rare and was made only in the seventeenth century from the famous fine Haarlem flax thread. Because the pattern is worked very closely it has a thick strong look (see figure 71). The design was

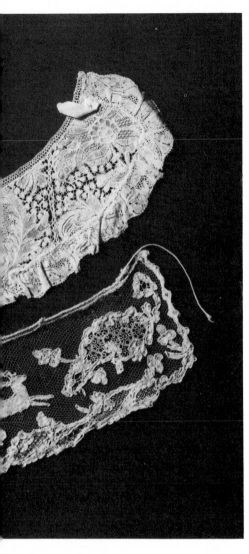

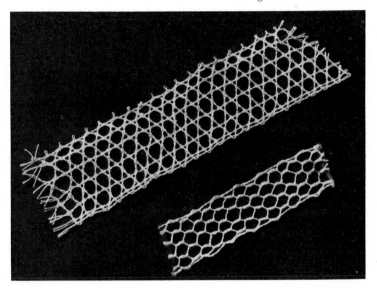

usually of formal flower heads. The lace was nearly all pattern work with very little grounding. It is fairly easy to recognise because the pattern work appears to be identical either side of a central line.

Flemish: Eighteenth Century
This differed from the earlier lace in that it had a Valenciennes ground. The ground and pattern were worked separately, the threads of the ground often being carried across the back of the pattern, which was usually scrolling.

Binche: Seventeenth and Eighteenth Centuries
Binche lace has a fine filmy texture and resembles that of early Valenciennes. It generally has no cordonnet, but if one is used it is very inconspicuous, being of the same thickness as the lace thread itself. The designs are complex and sometimes indefinite. The ground is usually a variety of *fond de neige* (snow ground). In some ways Binche is similar to Brussels, but Binche has more filling stitches in the design, and the ground is more varied. (See figure 72 (top).) In its later years, the Binche industry mostly made bobbin flowers for Brussels appliqué lace. Binche lace today is called *point de fee*.

Antwerp: Seventeenth, Eighteenth and Nineteenth Centuries
Antwerp lace was made all in one piece on the pillow. It has a cordonnet of untwisted thread and *point de paris* (kat stitch) or *cinque trous* (five hole) ground. The best known lace is *potten kant* (pot lace) because the designs always contained a vase of flowers or a flowerpot in some form. The early pot lace depicted the Annunciation.

The angel Gabriel was shown either with lilies in his hand or with a vase of flowers close by. Eventually Gabriel disappeared, but the vase of flowers remained.

Point d'Angleterre (English Point): Seventeenth and Eighteenth Centuries

The ground and pattern of this lace were made separately. It had beautiful designs of lilies, carnations and pomegranates. Also depicted were animals, human figures and Annunciation scenes.

In the seventeenth century examples there was no ground; the designs filled the whole area of the lace. In the eighteenth century the typical Brussels ground developed, consisting of a hexagonal mesh with two sides plaited and two sides twisted twice (see figure 73 (bottom)). This ground was almost identical to that of Mechlin except that the plaited sides were longer and the mesh, therefore, appeared slightly larger. This ground was known as *droschel* or *vrai reseau* (real ground). It was made in small strips and joined with *point de raccroc*, an invisible fine joining stitch.

FIGURE 74
Brussels lace lappets with *droschel* ground. Needlepoint insertions, circa 1750. Note the swans half way up

Extremely fine thread was used for this lace. There was no cordonnet; the edges and veins of the leaves and petals were raised by plaiting. Sometimes shading was achieved by alternating half stitches and whole stitches. Designs were in some ways similar to those of Valenciennes, but the texture was different in that Valenciennes was a perfectly flat fabric.

Brussels: Eighteenth Century

Motifs for this lace were made first and then linked together by the ground. (See figure 74.) The same hexagonal ground as that of *Point d'Angleterre* was used. By moving bobbins in a bunch from one part of a motif to another a raised edge was achieved. This technique gave a right and wrong side to the fabric because the twisted threads could be seen loose on the wrong side of the lace. There was no cordonnet as such. Very intricate fillings were used, and often they were needle-made.

Bruges (Duchess de Bruges): Nineteenth Century

This was a fairly coarse white guipure lace with the designs linked together by bars. The designs were not very imaginative, being mainly open flower heads and long trefoil leaves. It has a fairly definite cordonnet.

Brussels Duchesse: Nineteenth Century

This was a guipure lace similar to that of Bruges, but more artistic. It incorporated bold designs of flowers, often open primroses, and leaves. The leaves had prominent veins which were either plaited or oversewn. There was sometimes a cordonnet but it was not very prominent. The pattern was given some variety with whole stitches and half-stitches. (See figure 75.)

Brussels Mixed Lace (Duchesse de Bruxelles): Nineteenth Century

Brussels Mixed Lace was similar to *Duchesse* lace, except that it had small needle-made insertions, usually medallions.

Rosaline: Nineteenth Century

This was a guipure lace. It derived its

name from the simple rosebuds incorporated in the design. Whole stitches and half stitches were used in the pattern work. A late nineteenth century version had short, cloth stitch trails linking small flowers together.

Brussels Appliqué: Nineteenth Century

For this lace needle-made or bobbin-made motifs are appliquéed on to machine-made net. (See figures 76 and 77.)

France

Lille: Eighteenth and Nineteenth Centuries

Lille lace is easily recognizable by its very fine, light transparent ground known as *point de Lille (fond simple)*. The mesh is really diamond shaped but looks hexagonal because of the way it was made. On four sides two threads are twisted round each other, while on the other sides the threads are just loosely crossed. (See figure 78.) It had no plaited sides as did the Mechlin and Brussels grounds, and had a

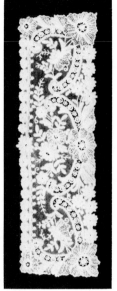

FIGURE 75
Top: Brussels *Duchesse* Mixed lace with raised rose, nineteenth century; bottom: Brussels *Duchesse* lace

FIGURE 76
Cuffs in Brussels mixed appliqué, nineteenth century

FIGURE 77
Brussels fan; nineteenth century

FIGURE 78
Lille or Bucks point
ground

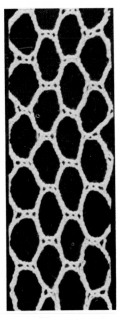

FIGURE 79
Round Valenciennes
ground

thick, flat untwisted cordonnet.

Old Lille lace had a straight edge and a rather stiff, formal pattern. The later Lille laces had patterns more like those of Mechlin, but Lille ground still retained the characteristic sprinkling of square dots (*point d'esprit*).

The mesh of eighteenth-century Lille lace was smaller than that of the nineteenth century variety. At the beginning of the nineteenth century the price of thread went up by a third, and the lace makers discovered they could save on thread by making a larger mesh.

Both black and white lace was made in Lille. In the eighteenth century a great deal of so-called 'Lille' lace was manufactured throughout Europe. It was referred to as '*migonettes*' or '*blondes de fil*'.

Lille and Arras laces were almost identical, except that Lille was a better quality lace and Arras was stronger and firmer to the touch, and very white. English Bucks point developed from Lille and Arras laces. Both Arras and Lille laces were made in a single piece.

Chantilly: Eighteenth and Nineteenth Centuries

Chantilly was a lace making district near Paris, but it also gave its name to a type of lace which was also produced in many other places. 'Chantilly' lace was produced in Le Puy, Bayeux, Caen and Calvados. A rather poorer type was produced in Buckinghamshire from 1860 to 1870, and acquired the name of 'Amersham Black'. Bayeux specialized in Chantilly shawls, and Caen in edgings. When large pieces were needed, the lace was made in sections and joined.

Chantilly was a black silk lace, but the silk used, which was known as grenadine, was not shiny but matt. It could have been taken for black thread. The pattern was usually half stitch surrounded by a cordonnet made of several strands of flat untwisted silk. The ground was either *fond Chant* or the hexagonal *point de Lille* (*fond simple*). The ground and pattern work were all of the same silk. Natural floral designs were typical of this lace: roses, tulips, irises, etc., with intertwining ribbons.

White Chantilly was made in the early

nineteenth century, from about 1805. Some was also reputed to have been made in the 1740s in flax thread, but virtually none of this early lace has survived.

Blondes: Eighteenth and Nineteenth Centuries

Blonde laces derived their name from the natural cream coloured silk from which they were originally made. Later, black and white blondes were also made. They were also called 'nankins'.

Blonde laces were made on the pillow in one operation. The typical ground was *point de Lille* (*fond simple*) with the pattern work outlined in a thick untwisted silk cordonnet. '*Blonde de Caen*' is said to have been made from about 1745. It was a brilliant white lace, its perfection rivalled only by that of Chantilly. White blondes were normally made only in the summer months, the black lace being made in the winter when fires, which were usually smoky and would have dirtied white lace, were needed for warmth.

Valenciennes: Seventeenth and Eighteenth Centuries

Valenciennes was a very rich looking lace made in one piece on the pillow. Very fine thread was used in its manufacture. It was a perfectly flat fabric and had no cordonnet.

Its distinctive ground had four plaited sides with no twists, and could be diamond shaped or round. The mesh helped to give the lace solidity. The pattern was made up of flowers and scrolls: carnations were popular. A feature of Valenciennes is that the pattern work is surrounded by tiny holes. (See figure 79.) Valenciennes mesh went through several phases before the plaited diamond-shaped mesh evolved. In some of the earlier laces *fond de neige* (snow ground) was used. The Flemish influence can also be detected in the early flower designs which included irises, tulips, lilies and anemones.

Lace of outstanding quality was being made in Valenciennes in the 1780s, but after that the lace began to deteriorate and the last worthwhile Valenciennes lace was made about 1840. Old Valenciennes lace was never really white – it always had a reddish tinge.

FIGURE 80
Black Chantilly lace
fan

FIGURE 81
Valenciennes lace,
property of Queen
Charlotte; eighteenth
century. Reproduced
by permission of
Castle Museum, York

FIGURE 82
Detail of
Valenciennes lace;
eighteenth century.
Note the outline of
small holes round
pattern work.
Reproduced by
permission of Castle
Museum, York

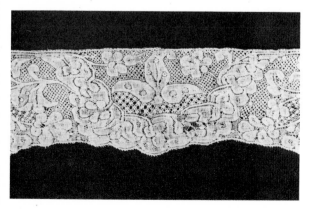

Mechlin (Malines): Seventeenth and Eighteenth Centuries

Mechlin was an extremely light, delicate lace. It was made all in one piece on the pillow. The ground was hexagonal with four sides twisted and two sides plaited. The twisted sides had two threads twisted twice and the plaited sides had four threads plaited three times. The ground looks similar to that of Brussels lace but the mesh is smaller because the plaited sides are shorter.

The chief characteristic of Mechlin lace was the flat, silky cordonnet with which the pattern was outlined. It gave the appearance of embroidery, and because of this Mechlin lace was sometimes called '*Broderie de Malines*'. The designs were usually floral, but a distinguishing feature was the scroll work which enclosed ornamental fillings and quatrefoils (four-leaf motifs). (See figure 84(5).) The lace normally had a straight edge. Occasionally Mechlin lace had an ornamental ground of *fond Chant* or *fond de neige* (snow ground) and *oeil de perdrix* (partridge eye) fillings, but this was not common.

Italy

Genoa: Seventeenth and Eighteenth Centuries

Genoese lace was very strong and solid. A characteristic of the lace was the deeply scalloped or vandyked edge joined to a narrow footing, and the wheatear or wheatgrain ornaments. The designs were geometrical and frequently had ribbons or trails of clothwork running through them which were joined together by bars. It was, therefore, a guipure lace. It was not until the seventeenth century that this lace became widely used throughout Europe when, because of its strength, it was used for boot-hose tops, scarves, collars and, in fact, anywhere that lace was required to stand up to hard wear.

Milan: Seventeenth and Eighteenth Centuries

In Milanese lace the patterns of scrolls and flowers were worked in fine, close clothwork with ornate fillings. The pattern work was connected by bars. In the early

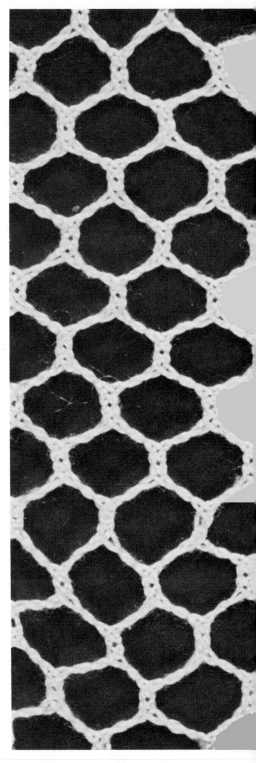

FIGURE 83
Detail, Mechlin ground

seventeenth century lace the bars were few, the flower heads being joined together where they touched. They fitted together like a beautiful jigsaw. Later seventeenth and early eighteenth century Milanese lace had the pattern work connected by bars with the addition of picots. (See figure 85.) The bars were usually arranged in pairs.

In the seventeenth century a Valenciennes type of round mesh was also made. (See figure 86.) Often the threads for the ground were carried across the back of the pattern work, and can easily be seen. The early laces have a fairly large mesh, but in later laces it is smaller. Other grounds besides Valenciennes were sometimes used in Milanese lace.

When Milanese lace was made to celebrate a particular family occasion such as a wedding, the family coat of arms or badge was sometimes woven into it.

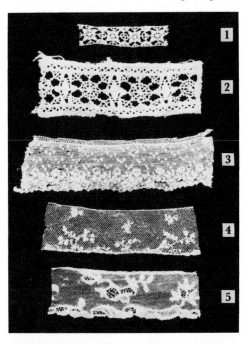

FIGURE 84
(1) Italian cutwork;
(2) *Reticella*; (3) *Point d'Alençon*; (4) *Point d'Argentan*;
(5) Mechlin

FIGURE 84A
Genoese bobbin lace. Nineteenth century copy of mid-seventeenth century lace

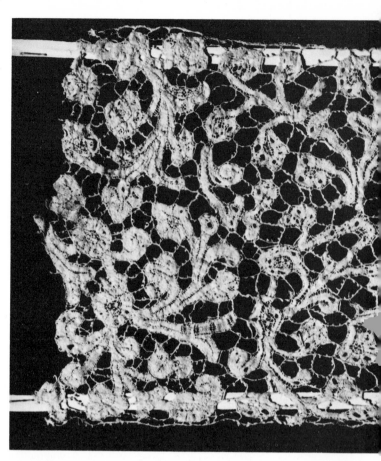

FIGURE 85
Milanese lace, late
seventeenth century.
Reproduced by
permission of Norfolk
Museums Service,
Norwich

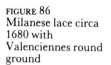
Milanese lace circa
1680 with
Valenciennes round
ground

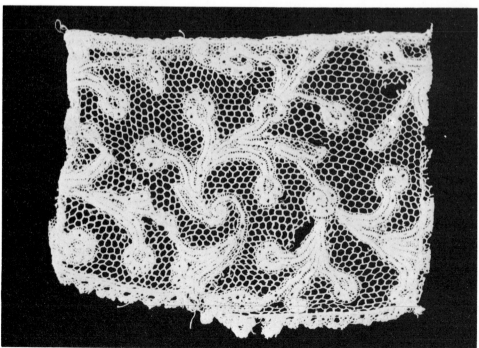

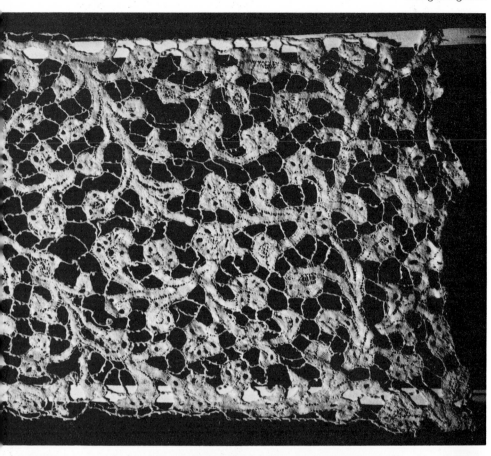

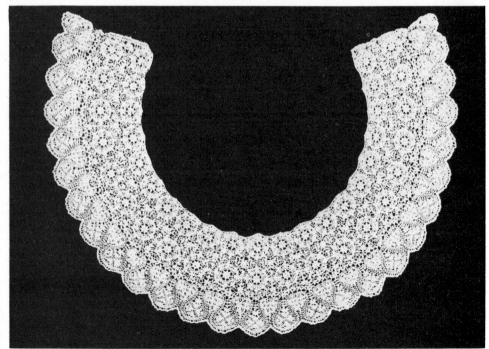

FIGURE 87
Cream Maltese silk
lace collar, nineteenth
century

FIGURE 88
(1) Cluny bobbin
lace; (2)
Northamptonshire
bobbin edging (baby
lace); (3) Corraline
needlepoint lace

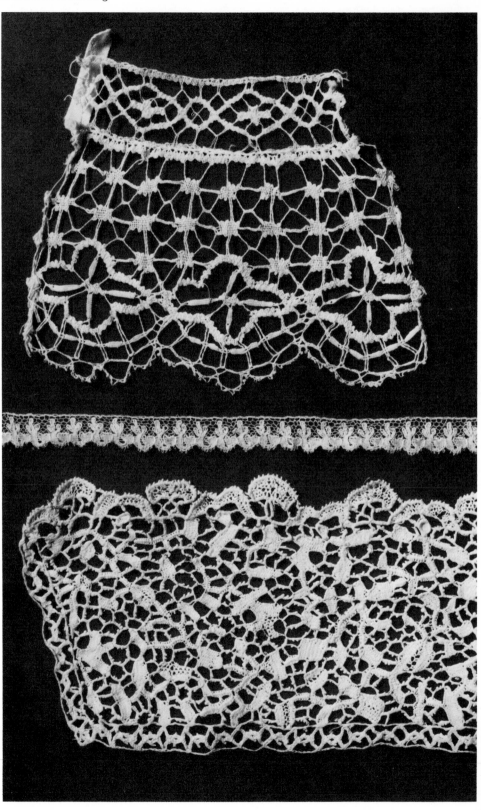

Malta

Maltese lace, made in the nineteenth century, developed from, and was similar to, that of Genoa. Its designs were geometrical with wheatear ornaments, and often a large number of leaves. The main feature of Maltese lace was the Maltese cross worked with the same basketwork stitch as the wheatears. It was a guipure lace, the pattern work being connected by bars. It usually had clothwork trails, which were not divided as they were in Cluny lace. The edge was usually finished with ninepin stitch. The lace was normally made of black or deep cream silk. Towards the end of the nineteenth century it was very popular for shawls, collars and cuffs.

Cluny

Cluny lace, also manufactured during the nineteenth century, was copied from some old Italian lace which was preserved in the Musée de Cluny, Paris, and hence its name. It was similar to Genoese and Maltese lace, being a lace of strong geometrical design. It had designs of scallops and wheatears, but differed from Maltese lace in that the trails were divided. The pattern work was joined by plaited bars, usually with picots, and it had a distinctive twisted footside. The edge differed from that of Maltese because it had a sixpin rather than a ninepin stitch border. (See figures 88(1) and 89.) It was adapted and made in England during the second half of the nineteenth century. It was a heavy duty lace suitable for curtains, tablecloths and other furnishings.

England

Torchon: Nineteenth Century

This lace was made on the Continent in the sixteenth and seventeenth centuries,

FIGURE 89
Late nineteenth century nightdress made completely by hand with Cluny edgings and insertions

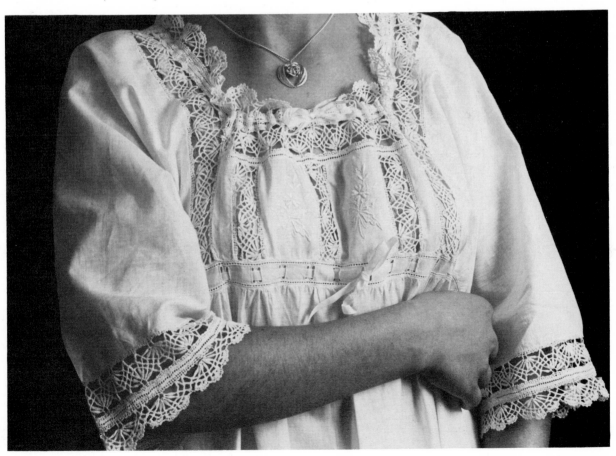

FIGURE 90
Torchon edgings and
insertion, early
twentieth century

and was called 'beggar's lace'. It was made in England at the end of the nineteenth century, and became popular when handmade lace was competing with that of the machines. The name Torchon was derived from the French word for rag or dishcloth. It was a geometric lace with a simple twisted ground. There was no cordonnet. Lozenge and spider patterns and fan edging were typical. Sometimes tallies and wheatears were also included, and half stitch and whole stitch were used. (See figures 90, 91 and 92.) Some very attractive patterns can be found in Torchon lace and it is sometimes unfairly maligned.

Bucks: Eighteenth and Nineteenth Centuries

Bucks (short for Buckinghamshire) lace

FIGURE 91
Detail of Torchon ground

FIGURE 92
Modern Torchon edged mat, made by a young child

FIGURE 93
Buckinghamshire
lace, early nineteenth
century

FIGURE 94
Baby's gown with
white eyelet
embroidery and
insertions of Bucks
lace, circa 1880

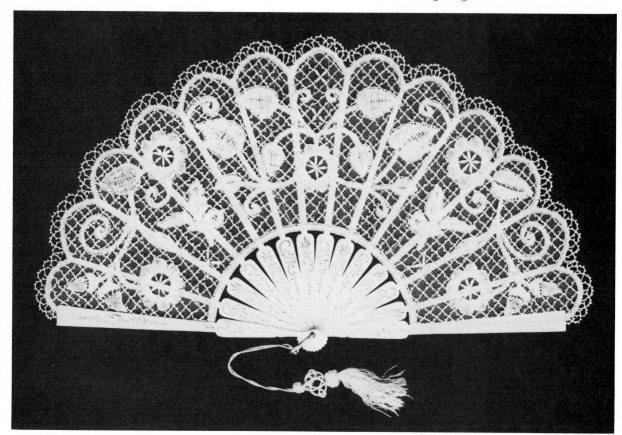

FIGURE 95
Bedfordshire lace fan
mounted on net,
nineteenth century

was not confined to Bucks alone. This was the name given to all English lace with a *point de Lille* (*fond simple*) ground, but it was mainly made in the East Midland counties of Buckinghamshire, Bedfordshire and Northamptonshire. The lace was worked continuously in one piece on the pillow. Kat stitch (*point de Paris*) and Mechlin grounds were also used. The Lille ground was sprinkled with dots (*point d'esprit*) and a thick soft gimp outlined the pattern work. (See figure 93 and 94.)

Bucks lace designs were either repetitive floral or softly geometrical ones as in the fan patterns (figure 97) which was a rounded triangle, or as in the single or double ring patterns which were circles and ovals. Geometric patterns were mainly used for edgings and insertions, while the non-geometrical floral patterns, adapted from Mechlin designs, were used for flounces. Typical Mechlin designs were those with scrolls which ran along the headside enclosing various fillings such as

mayflower, honeycomb or wireground. Typical Lille designs were floral sprigs scattered over the Lille mesh. The patterns had names which usually referred to some part of the design, such as honeysuckle, convolvulus, rose, queen's garter, or duke's garter.

Beds-Maltese: Nineteenth Century

Today this lace is sometimes referred to simply as 'Beds'. It was introduced in the nineteenth century, and was first shown at the Great Exhibition of 1851. As it was made so much more quickly than Bucks point ground lace, Bedfordshire lace was introduced in order to compete with machine-made lace which was coming on to the market in large quantities.

Maltese was a guipure lace based on Maltese designs. (See figures 95 and 96.) The pattern work was joined by plaited bars which were decorated by picots. It had a scalloped edge typically finished with a ninepin border or with picots. Like

Maltese it had wheatears, but the ends were squared, not tapered as in Maltese. A typical Midland name for these was 'barleycorn'. Some designs had a winding clothwork trail which, unlike Cluny, was never divided. One type of Beds-Maltese lace had plaited flowers linked together by a loose torchon ground. (See figure 98(b).)

Yak: Nineteenth Century
This lace, originally produced from yak hair, was made in England from worsted in the late nineteenth century. Patterns were mainly Torchon or Maltese, sometimes with *cinq trous* (five-hole) ground. Being very heavy and thick, it was used mainly to trim capes, winter dresses and furniture. Its popularity was short-lived.

Devon (Honiton): Eighteenth and Nineteenth Centuries
This lace differed from the Midlands laces in that the motifs and ground were made separately as in Brussels lace. It was a dainty lace made of fine thread, and was used especially for wedding veils and gowns. (See figures 99, 100 and 101.)

The motifs were typically butterflies, roses, flower sprays, shamrocks, thistles and sometimes birds and fishes. They were worked in whole stitch or half stitch and have a wide variety of very charming fillings with names such as 'toad in the hole', 'blossom', 'cartwheel', 'snatch bar' and 'Jubilee'. Sometimes the motifs were flat and outlined with a silky cordonnet, or the edges were raised and rolled as in

FIGURE 96
Bedfordshire-Maltese lace, late nineteenth century

FIGURE 97
Baby lace fan edging
(Bucks point)

Brussels lace.

The ground varied; it could be bobbin-made mesh, or bride ground with picots. In the older laces there was a needle-made ground resembling that of Alençon lace. Eighteenth-century Devon lace sometimes had a true *droschel* ground. Nineteenth-century lace was usually made by appliquéed motifs on machine-made three-twist net. In the hand-made bobbin ground the threads were seldom carried across the back of the motifs as they were in the Italian Milanese lace.

Italy and Flanders

Tape Lace: Seventeenth Century

Tape lace was produced from woven or bobbin-made tape formed into patterns and linked together by bars. An early seventeenth-century form tried to imitate Venetian needlepoint lace, but the result was rather stiff and clumsy as the bends and gathers in the tape could be easily seen. Later tape laces were much more attractive, for the tape varied in width and was shaped to fit the pattern without the need for folds. (See figures 102 and 103.)

FIGURE 98
(a) Daisy insertion with coloured daisies, made by Winslow Lace Industry; early twentieth century; (b) Beds-Maltese lace with Torchon ground; (c) Torchon with leaves

FIGURE 99
Honiton lace collar
and cuffs with bride
ground, eighteenth
century

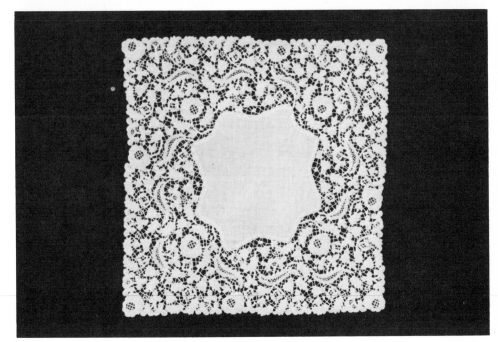

FIGURE 100
Honiton lace with
bride ground,
eighteenth century

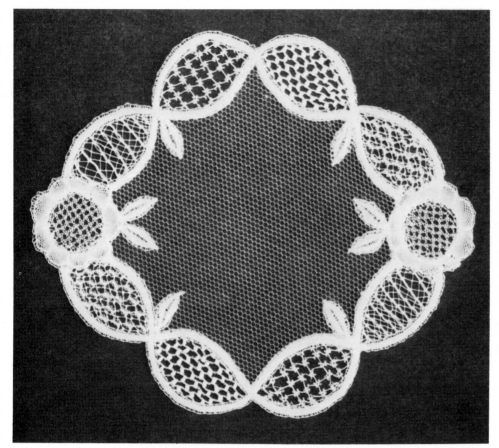

FIGURE 101
Modern Honiton lace
mat with appliqué

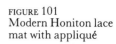
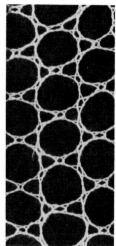

FIGURE 103
Detail of a fancy
ground, *point de
mariage*

FIGURE 102
Tape lace in the
making. Bobbin-
made tape being
joined by needle-
made bars and
fillings, seventeenth
century

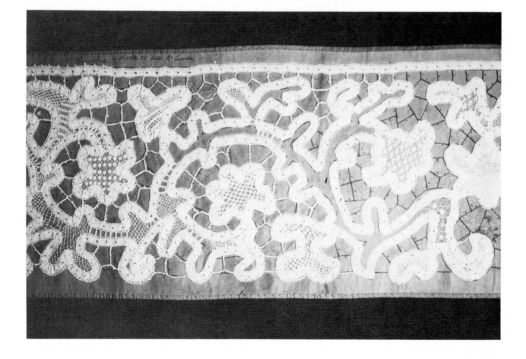

NEEDLEPOINT LACE

Needlepoint lace was made with a sewing needle and thread using an ordinary button-hole stitch. It was fundamentally an embroidery, while bobbin lace was basically weaving.

The earliest needlepoint lace was called 'cutwork' in England and *Reticella* in Italy. It was made by cutting away squares of material and filling the spaces with embroidery. The result was a strictly geometrical design. In early *reticella* the spaces were filled with simple buttonhole bars and picots, but the later laces had more ornate bars and the patterns were much more solid, with wheels, circles and triangles. This type of lace was made mostly in Italy but some was made in England in the sixteenth and early seventeenth centuries. It was used for church vestments and for ruffs, cuffs and collars.

(See figure 84(1) and (2).)

Reticella developed into the needlepoint laces which were made on parchment without fabric. The Italians called it *punto in aria* (stitches in the air). It was worked in the following way. The design was first drawn on parchment and then carefully outlined by threads, which were also stitched right through the linen. The next step was to fill in all the solid parts of the design with buttonhole stitching and work the ornamental filling stitches. When all this was completed, the motifs were finally linked together with bars or a looped mesh. The lace was released from the parchment by passing a knife through the two thicknesses of linen.

A small wicker basket or cushion was used to support the parchment pattern and lace while it was being worked. This is why confusion can occur if bobbin lace is termed 'pillow' lace.

FIGURE 104
Top: Venetian *Gros Point*, repaired with net insertions; bottom: Flemish lace using the round Valenciennes ground, early nineteenth century

FIGURE 105
Venice points: *Gros Point* and rose points, seventeenth century

Italy

There were six main Italian needlepoint laces, three flat and three raised and padded. The three flat laces, which preceded the padded ones, were Venetian Flat Point (*Point Plat de Venise*), Grounded Venice Point (*Point de Venise à Réseau*) and Corraline Point. The three raised laces were Venetian Gros Point, Venetian Rose (Raised) Point and Venetian Point de Neige.

Venetian Gros Point: Sixteenth and Seventeenth Centuries

This was a very bold lace with large motifs which sometimes measured as much as 5 cm (2 in.) across. It was very raised and padded with a wide cordonnet. The motifs were joined together by short bars decorated with picots. The whole appearance of the lace resembled carved ivory.

Venetian Rose (Raised) Point: Sixteenth and Seventeenth Centuries

This lace was really a smaller version of Gros point except that the flowers were smaller and less padded, and usually built up in layers or tiers. The linking bars were much more elaborate.

Venetian Point de Neige: Sixteenth and Seventeenth Centuries

This was a very elaborate form of Venetian Rose point and once seen it can never be mistaken. The flowers were still tiered and there was a prominent cordonnet. An abundance of picots surrounded the flowers with geometric precision and were often worked in tiny scallops. Little rosettes were worked on the bars (*brides picotées et rosacées*). It was an exceptionally beautiful and elaborate lace.

Venetian Flat Point: Sixteenth and Seventeenth Centuries

As the name implies, there was no padding to this lace; other than this, it was similar to the raised laces. The flowers and scrolls were closely worked and had a large variety of ornate fillings. The bars were decorated with picots. There was no cordonnet.

Coraline Point: Seventeenth, Eighteenth and Nineteenth Centuries

This was a variety of Venetian flat point. It was referred to as 'mermaid's lace'. The pattern was very irregular and joined together by bars. This lace was easily copied by machinery in the nineteenth century. (See figure 88(3).)

Grounded Venice Point: Early Eighteenth Century

Very few specimens of this lace survive today. The delicate pattern and cobweb thread did not stand up to wear and tear. It had a very fine mesh ground similar to that of Alençon needlepoint. The design was a fairly formal one of flowers with a flat cordonnet stitched round the edge of the pattern work. A minute border of tiny squares separated the ground from the pattern.

Burano: Eighteenth and Nineteenth Centuries

This lace was made in Burano in the eighteenth century, but little of it survived. It resembled grounded Venice point, except that it was a stronger lace, although still made with very fine thread. It had a flat cordonnet and a square mesh. The Burano industry died out and was later revived. The lace school established there specialized in copying old pieces of lace. Alençon, *point d'Angleterre*, Argentan and Brussels were all imitated. These imitations can be mistaken for genuine old pieces.

FIGURE 106
Hollie Point cap, eighteenth century

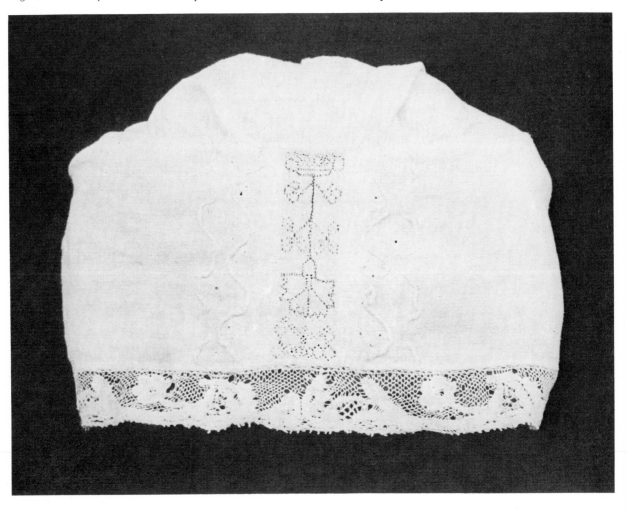

The modern Burano point of the nineteenth century was a soft cotton lace with comparatively more ground than pattern. The latter was a twisted looped ground similar to that of *point d'Alençon*, but the unevenness of the cotton thread gave the ground a cloudy appearance. Its inconspicuous cordonnet, which was oversewn, helps to distinguish it from *point d'Alençon*, which had the cordonnet held in place by close buttonholing, and from *point de Gaze*, which had spaced buttonholing.

France

Point d'Alençon: Seventeenth and Eighteenth Centuries

Point d'Alençon was one of the principle needlepoint laces of France. It was known as *point de France* until the late seventeenth century, when it became known as *point d'Alençon*, although this name for the lace was not widely used in England.

The industry was established by Colbert in the 1650s and the first lace was made indistinguishable from the Venetian points, owing to the influence of the Italian immigrant workers. In the late seventeenth century the lace changed its character and became altogether a lighter and more delicate lace with a clearly defined pattern.

The ground of *Point d'Alençon* appeared square rather than hexagonal and was worked with a double twisted thread over horizontal threads, which gave the appearance of rows of lines or holes. The most important feature of the lace was the very prominent cordonnet, which was of horse hair worked over with fine buttonhole stitches. This cordonnet was peculiar to *Point d'Alençon*, and was not found in any other lace except Argentan, which was closely linked to *point d'Alençon*. The lace also had exceptionally beautiful fillings. (See figure 72 (bottom).) It was made in small pieces and joined with a seam following the pattern outlines wherever possible. This was a different method from the fine joining stitch used to join the ground work in other laces and which formed another row of stitching.

In the nineteenth century *Point d'Alençon* was made in Burano, Brussels and Bayeux as well as in Alençon.

Argentella: Seventeenth and Eighteenth Centuries

This was a rare lace, a variety of *Point d'Alençon*. Its ground of solid hexagons within skeletal hexagons filled the spaces between the pattern work, which was mainly floral.

Point d'Argentan: Seventeenth and Eighteenth Centuries

The distinguishing feature of *Point d'Argentan* lace was its very large hexagonal bride ground. Each side of the very strong ground was worked over with seven or eight fine buttonhole stitches. These do not appear in any other lace. Occasionally some of the brides were fringed with three or four little picots. It had a flat cordonnet, and the patterns were floral with scrolls and ribands. The early eighteenth-century lace was more pattern work than ground. (See figure 84(4).)

Belgium

Point de Gazé: Late Nineteenth to Early Twentieth Century

Point de Gazé developed from eighteenth century *Point de Brussels*, of which there is very little left. *Point de Gazé* was a lovely, light, airy lace. It was made of fine thread, and the ground of looped threads without twists contributed to the delicacy of the fabric. Typical pattern work was of roses with layered petals, twining ribands and scrolls. A cordonnet was sewn on with spaced buttonhole stitches, and many attractive fillings were used.

England

Hollie Point: Sixteenth, Seventeenth and Eighteenth Centuries

Hollie, or holy, point was so called because the designs were usually biblical: the Lamb of God, the Tree of Knowledge, the Holy Dove and the Annuniciation, the last being usually represented by a lily or carnation. The name was also appropriate because the lace was used mainly for infants' christening sets. Insertion strips of hollie point were sewn along the shoulders of the gowns and down the backs of the linen caps and bonnets. Mittens and cuffs were also decorated with this lace.

18 Mounting, Washing and Mending Lace

Mounting

When mounting new lace, or re-mounting old lace, be careful to select the right weight of fabric for the lace. If the fabric is too heavy it will tear the lace, and if it is too light the lace will pull away from it. Either way the appearance of the lace will be spoilt.

Always remember that machine-made lace may be attached to the fabric by machines or by hand, but hand-made lace must never be attached by machine!

In figure 107 the machine-made lace has been sewn on with a zig-zag machine stitch. Any fancy machine stitch looks attractive, but one that swings from side to side is more attractive than a straight one.

FIGURE 107
Machine lace sewn on with machine zig-zag stitch

FIGURE 108
Braid sewn on with three-sided punch stitch. Lace sewn to braid. Lace is Beds-Maltese with Torchon ground

A good method of attaching hand-made lace is to make a narrow braid or footing as in figure 70. Sew this to the fabric first of all, and then attach the lace to the braid. The fabric often wears out before the lace, and by using this method the lace can be removed without spoiling it. The footing is part of the lace and should always be laid over the fabric on the right side to its full depth. The fabric behind the footing is cut away after the lace has been sewn on. If possible, try to use the same thread as that of the lace, as the footing will then merge in with the fabric.

In figure 109 the lace has been attached by hand with a whip stitch. In figure 110 it has been sewn on with a three-sided punch stitch; this takes a little longer but gives the lace a professional finish. The stitch consists of a row of triangles outlined in back stitch and results in a row of attractive little perforations. It is worked by taking a double back stitch through three holes in a triangle, using a thick punch needle and pulling the thread tightly. An excellent way of keeping the holes straight is to pull a single thread as shown in figure 108. This also helps to emphasize the row of holes. Diagram 29 makes the method of working clear. A similar four-sided stitch can also be used.

Washing

If lace is very old, don't wash it unless absolutely necessary as it may disintegrate!

Before washing any lace be sure you know what it is made of. Silk and coloured lace must not be washed in soap powder containing bleach, or in very hot water. Linen and cotton will stand up to very hot, even boiling, water.

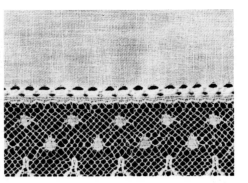

FIGURE 109
Detail: lace sewn on with whip stitch

FIGURE 110
Detail: lace sewn on with three-sided punch stitch, or Turkish stitch

There are several methods of washing. The old lace makers stitched white flannel or a thick cloth round a bottle, carefully wound the lace around it and stitched the ends. It was then gently washed and rinsed by hand and the bottle turned upside down over a stick in the garden. The lace was left to dry and bleach in the sun. The old lace makers called this 'hazelling' the lace.

One modern way is to use a large glass jar with a wide neck and a screw top. Use a strong plastic jar if you are going to use very hot water, as glass can crack. Fill the jar about half full of soapy water, put in the lace and screw on the top, and gently shake until the lace is clean. Rinse in the same way.

If large pieces of lace are to be washed, make a bag from old curtain net, butter muslin or cheese cloth. Put the lace in the bag and tack the top together, then squeeze gently by hand in soap suds. Alternatively, the lace can be stitched carefully into shape on white cloth and washed in the same way, but be careful not to catch it on jewellery or rings. This is a good method if you wish to boil it. Never be tempted to put lace into a washing machine!

To dry, pin the lace very carefully into shape with rustless pins on a board padded with thick white cloth. Pins should be put in all round the headside and along the footside. Every picot should have a pin as well as key places where threads cross. Take a good look at the lace before you begin to wash it and you should be able to judge where to put the pins. Leave the lace in place until it is perfectly dry. Sunshine is a good whitener, so put it outdoors whenever possible, but watch for marauding cats!

Mending

Mending torn lace is a very skilled job so try to get it repaired by an expert. Your local lace school or guild will have a register of people who can mend lace, and will let you have their names and addresses if you send appropriate postage.

Do remember that all lace cannot be repaired successfully. Very old lace was made with extremely fine thread which cannot be obtained today, and any repair will show. Modern laces do not present quite such a problem, and a skilled lace maker can probably work a new piece of ground, or even re-ground the lace altogether, but with the time and skill involved this might be expensive.

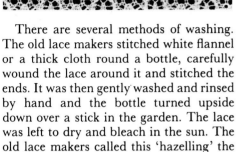

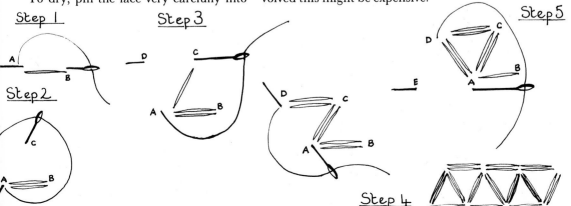

Glossary

Appliqué Motifs sewn on to a net background

Baby lace Narrow lace edgings (E. Midlands term)

Bars Narrow plaits or threads linking together motifs in a design

Bertha A very deep cape-like collar worn with a low necked dress

Blonde lace Lace made with silk in black, white or cream

Bobbin Elongated spool used as a handle to manipulate threads and also for winding the thread on

Bone lace, Bone work Old names for bobbin lace

Borders Edging narrower than flounces, usually for gathering

Brides See bars and Appendix

Brides picotées Bars ornamented with picots (bobbin lace)

Buttonhole stitch Main stitch in needlepoint lace

Candle block, Candle stool Tall stool for holding candles and flashes for lighting purposes

Chain lace Tambour lace

Cloth stitch Complete stitch in bobbin lace. See Appendix

Cloth work Linen-like weaving in bobbin lace. See Appendix

Cordonnet Heavy thread for outlining patterns

Cutwork Early lace made by cutting away the material and filling in with embroidery

Darned net Embroidery on machine-made lace or filet lace

Droschel Flemish word for special bobbin-made ground in Brussels and *Point d'Angleterre* lace

Dots Spots sprinkled on Lille ground. See Appendix

Down Full length of a parchment pattern (about 35 cm, 14 in.)

Duchesse Nineteenth century guipure lace (Belgian)

Eches Cotton or linen tabs sewn on to the ends of a parchment pattern

Filet lace Darned patterns on square mesh

Fillings Fancy stitches used in the centre of enclosed spaces. See Appendix

Flounce Wide lace made in a continuous strip

Flash cushion Straw cushion for supporting flasks

Flask, flash Glass globes for magnifying light

Fond See ground and Appendix

Footing Narrow edge which is sewn on to material. See Appendix

Gingles Bands of pewter, etc., round bobbins

Groppo Knot, tie (Italian)

Ground Mesh or bars which join and support the pattern. See Appendix

Guipure lace Originally a lace made with narrow strips of parchment whipped over

with gold or silver thread.
Modern meaning is a bold lace linked together
  with bars and no mesh.
Half stitch   An openwork stitch in bobbin
  lace
Head, headside   Fancy edge of lace. See
  Appendix
Hutch   A basket for holding spare flasks
Insertion   Lace with straight edges on both
  sides, both edges being attached to material
Lacis   See filet lace
Lappets   Long, narrow decorative pieces
  hanging from the sides of a head-dress. Made
  in pairs
Leads   Sheets of lead on which parchments
  were pricked
Mat, matt   Clothwork of flowers, etc.
Motif   Sprig or spray made separately in
  some laces, and joined together afterwards
Needlepoint   Lace made with a needle and
  built up with buttonhole stitches
Oeil de perdrix   Also partridge eye.
  Ornamental ground of a solid hexagon inside
  a skeleton hexagon
Passement   Early name for lace
Pearl, purl   Picot, tiny loop on bars or edges
Pereline   A very deep collar fashionable in
  the nineteenth century
Pillow horse, Pillow maid   Stand for
  supporting lace pillow
Pillow lace   Old name for bobbin lace
Point lace   Needlepoint lace but also used for

especially fine quality bobbin lace
Points   See point lace
Punto in aria   Italian for early needle lace
  with no linen foundation (literally meaning
  stitches in the air)
Purling   Stitch for uniting sprigs in Honiton
  lace
Quill   Bobbin with a long neck for winding
  on gimp before winding it on to a trolly
  bobbin.
Raccroc   Fine joining stitch used for joining
  droschel ground invisibly
Réseau   French for ground. See Appendix
Setting in   Beginning a pattern in bobbin lace
Setting up   Moving up the lace after a
  complete down has been worked
Spangles   Glass beads used to weight bobbins
Tallies   Dots. See Appendix
Toilé   The pattern or solid clothwork parts of
  bobbin or needlepoint lace
Trolly bobbin   Buckinghamshire name for
  bobbin carrying gimp
Trolly lace   Buckinghamshire name for lace
  outlined with gimp or Devonshire lace made
  with a coarse thread and worked
  continuously round and round the pillow
Rounds   Shaped parts for babies bonnets,
  caps, etc.
Wheatears, Wheat grains   Ornaments of
  closely worked basket stitch as seen in
  Maltese, Beds-Maltese and
  Genoese laces

Appendix

Single ground, also: Point ground
Point de Lille
Lille ground
Point simple
Fond claire
Fond simple

Double ground also: Wire ground
Kat stitch ground
French ground
Six pointed star ground
Fond chant (short for
  Chantilly)
Point de Paris
Point double
Fond double
Point des champs

Snow (snowy) *Punto neve* (Italian)
ground also: *Point de neige* (French)

Dots also: Spots
Plaits
Point d'esprit
Tallies
Leadwork

Fillings also: *Modes*
Jours

Footing also: Footside
Engrêlure

Ground also: *Fond*
Champ
Réseau

Bars also: *Brides*
Pearl (purl) ties
Legs
Straps
Coxcombs
Bridges

Clothwork also: Close work
Toilé
Fondo a tela (Italian)

Headside also: Head
Heading
Pearl (purl) or picot edge
Turnside (Bucks)
Dykeside (when edge is
  vandyked)

Cloth stitch also: Close stitch
Linen stitch

Needle-made lace Needlepoint
also: *Point à l'aiguille* (French)
Punto in aco (Italian)

Bibliography

ALFORD, Lady M., *Needlework as an Art*, E. P. Publishing Ltd, 1975.

ALLEN, W. G., *John Heathcoat and His Heritage*, Johnson, 1957.

ARNOLD, J., *A Handbook of Costume*, Macmillan, London, 1973.

BROOKE, M. L., *Lace in the Making with Bobbins and Needle*, Routledge & Kegan Paul, London, 1923.

Castle Museum, *Nottingham Lace*, Castle Museum Publications, Nottingham.

CHANNER, C., *Lace Making Point Ground*, Dryad, Leicester, 1953.

CLOSE, E., *Lace Making*, John Gifford, London, 1970.

CUNNINGHAM, W. & C., *Handbook of English Costume 17th Century*, Faber & Faber, London, 1954.

CUNNINGHAM, C. W. & P. E. & BEARD, *Dictionary of English Costume*, A. C. Black, London, 1960.

COLLIER, A., *Lace*, Kingsclere Publications, Reading, 1979.

DRUK, DERDE, *Kant*, Rijksmuseum Amsterdam, 1960.

EARNSHAW, PAT, *The Identification of Lace*, Shire Publications, 1980.

FELKIN, W. A., *History of the Machine-Wrought Hosiery and Lace Manufacturers*, David & Charles, 1961.

FREEMAN, C., *Pillow Lace in the East Midlands*, Luton Museum and Art Gallery, 1958.

GROVES, S., *A History of Needlework Tools and Accessories*, Country Life Ltd, London, 1966.

HALLS, Z., *Machine Made Lace in Nottingham*, City of Nottingham Museum & Art Gallery, 1971.

Harrods Ltd, *Victorian Shopping (1895)*, David & Charles, 1972.

HAWKINS, D. W., *Old Point Lace*, Chatters & Windus, 1878.

HENNEBERG, F. A., *The Art & Craft of Old Lace*, Batsford, London, 1931.

HOPEWELL, J., *Pillow Lace and Bobbins*, Shire Publications, Aylesbury, Bucks, 1977.

HUETSON, T. L., *Lace & Bobbins History and Collector's Guide*, David & Charles, 1973.

HUNGERFORD, P., *Seven Centuries of Lace*, Heineman, 1908.

INDER, P. M., *Honiton Lace*, Exeter Museum Publications, 1971.

JACKSON, N., *History of Handmade Lace*, L. Upcott Gill, London, 1900.

JOURDAIN, M., *Old Lace*, Batsford, London, 1908.

KINMOND, J., *Anchor Book of Lace Crafts*, Batsford, London, 1961.

KLIOT, KOETHE, *Bobbin Lace formed by Twisting of Cords*, Allen & Unwin, 1973.

LAVER, J., *Costume in Detail*, Cassell, London, 1963.

LUXTON, E., *The Technique of Honiton Lace*, Batsford, 1979.

MAIDMENT, M., *Hand-Made Bobbin Lace Work*, Paul Minet, Chicheley, 1971.

MINCOFF & MARRIAGE, M. A., *Pillow Lace*, John Murray, 1907.

MORRIS, J. A., *The Art of Ayreshire White Needlework*, Glasgow, 1916.

MOUNTFIELD, A., *Shops and Shopping*, Wayland, 1976.

NOTTINGHAM, P., *The Technique of Bobbin Lace*, Batsford, London, 1976.

PALLISER, Mrs Bury, *A History of Lace*, 1875; Sampson Low, Marston & Co., 1902, republished by Ebury Press, London, 1980.

PETHEBRIDGE, J. E., *A Manual of Lace*, Cassell & Co, London, 1947.

PFANNSCHMIDT, *Twentieth Century Lace*, Mills & Boon, London, 1975.

POND, G., *An Introduction to Lace*, Garnstone Press, London, 1973.

SIMEON, Margaret, *The History of Lace*, Stainer & Bell, London, 1979.

SWAIN, M., *The Flowerers*, W. R. Chambers, London, n.d.

VINCIOLO, FREDERIC DI, *Renaissance Patterns for Lace and Embroidery*, Constable, London, 1971.

Museums with Lace Collections

Abingdon Museum, Abingdon Road, Northampton
Bedford Museum, The Embankment, Bedford
Birmingham City Museum and Art Gallery, Congreve Street, Birmingham
Buckinghamshire County Museum, Church Street Aylesbury, Bucks
Castle Museum, York
Cecil Higgins Art Gallery, Castle Close, Bedford (View by Appointment)
Cowper and Newton Museum, Market Place, Olney, Bucks
Gawthorpe Hall, Padiham, Lancs
Holly Trees, Colchester, Essex (Coggeshall lace)
Honiton and All Hallows Public Museum, High Street, Honiton, Devon

Museum of Costumes and Textiles, Castlegate, Nottingham
National Museum of Ireland, Kildare Street, Dublin
Royal Albert Memorial Museum and Art Gallery, Queen Street, Exeter
The Museum and Art Gallery, Wardown Park, Luton, Beds.
Waddeston Manor, Aylesbury, Bucks
Victoria and Albert Museum, South Kensington, London

Musée de la Dentelle, 4, 6, 8, rue de la Violette, B-1000 Bruxelles
Musée de l'Artisanat Malinois, Zoutwerf, B-2800 Mechelen (Malines)

Suppliers

United Kingdom

E. Braggins & Sons, 26–36 Silver Street, Bedford, Beds
Audrey Sells, 49 Pedley Lane, Clifton, Shefford, Beds
Mace & Nairn, 89 Crane Street, Salisbury, Wilts
Ye Honiton Lace Shoppe, 44 High Street, Honiton, Devon
Mary Allen, Wirksworth, Derbyshire (linen and threads only)
Paul Durst, The Keep, 5 West Wall Presteigne, Powys, Wales (bobbins and winders – bobbins made to personal design)

United States

Lacis, 2990 Adeline Street, Berkeley, California 94703
Frederick J. Fawcett Inc., 129 South Street, Boston, Mass 02111 (threads)
Osma Galliger Tod, 319 Mendoza Avenue, Coral Gables, Florida 33134

Australia

Stadia Handcrafts, 85 Elizabeth Street, Paddington, N.S.W. 2021
Spindle & Loom, Arcade 83 Longueville Road, Lane Cove, Sydney 2066
The Lacemaker, 94 Fordham Avenue, Hartwell, Victoria 3124

Index